Pneuma Life is incredibly well-written, accessible, insightful, and deeply encouraging. Sue Boldt has done an amazing job of unpacking what it means to be a believer who lives in the fullness of all that God has provided for us by the Holy Spirit. She has done this in a way that is both biblically accurate and practically understood. As a pastor, I see the need for excellent resources like Pneuma Life; for individuals as well as those in small groups who are seeking the fullness of the Spirit. I love this book because Sue Boldt loves the church and wants every believer to know and walk in the Holy Spirit's power and presence!

Pastor Brian Goodell, MASL
Senior Pastor, The Bridge Foursquare Church
ICFG Regional Pastor, NorCal Region

If you are looking for a practical and insightful study of the Holy Spirit, look no further than Pneuma Life. Sue Boldt's creative writing style and in-depth analysis of scripture bring a clear and concise understanding of the Third Person of The Trinity. Laid out in Bible study format, Pneuma Life is perfect for an individual or small group study.

Rob McKenna
Senior Pastor, Bridge South Bay, CA

Sue Boldt's eye-opening book, Pneuma Life, will help you grow and understand the work and person of the Holy Spirit. Practical and insightful, it will help you walk in and use the tools God has given us through His Holy Spirit, equipping you to walk in your God-given authority.

Cindy Fry
The Rock Church, Danville, CA

"For the sake of a dying, weary world that needs to see God's power and love on display..." **Pneuma Life** *leaps from the lofty heights of theory into the present reality of the miraculous, divinely empowered life the Lord intends for His followers to live. Upon His resurrection, Jesus did not leave us alone to navigate this life; He left us Himself in the person of the Holy Spirit, and Sue Boldt masterfully guides us along the biblical path to discover all He has for us. Her book imparts a life-changing message as she infuses her readers with faith and the expectation of stepping into the fullness of the extraordinary, miraculous life God intends for His people to live through the power of the Holy Spirit, all for His glory.*

Maureen Broderson
Pastor, Teacher, Author
Victorious Spiritual Warfare, So Simple, Grandma Can Do It

I would like to congratulate Sue Boldt for giving us this in-depth masterpiece on how to interact with the Holy Spirit. This teaching will benefit the new believer as each chapter reveals the ministry of the Holy Spirit, discloses God's power to protect our testimony, and shows us how to live godly lifestyles above everyday temptations. **Pneuma Life** *is also beneficial to assist the seasoned believer seeking to refine their relationship with God and to reach another dimension of connection. What really stirred my spirit was how each chapter was a reminder of God's love made available to me in cultivating my relationship with the person of the Holy Spirit. Thank you, Sue, for this priceless gem to equip the Body of Christ and show us how to stay closely connected to the Holy Spirit, which is our best opportunity to succeed in life.*

Todd E. Clease
Senior Pastor NewLife LA
ICFG Regional Pastor, SoCal Region

Pneuma Life is an excellent discipleship tool. I've used Sue's original book many times to disciple believers who lacked an understanding of who the Holy Spirit is and the role He plays in their lives. From the Old to New Testaments, Sue teaches about the life-changing power the Holy Spirit wants to give and that every believer needs both inwardly for their life and outwardly for their ministry. It's so rewarding as I sit with those I pray with and watch the "lights turn on" as the Spirit of God fills them with His power and leads them into a deeper relationship with Him.

Linda Stanley
Office Administrator
New Life Church, Pomona, CA

I didn't have my prayer language and I didn't know how to get it, but I was so hungry for it. Who is the Holy Spirit? Who is He for me? Who is He in the Bible? Who was He then, and who is He now? I found the answers to these questions in the original **Pneuma Life**. *Through the study and receiving an understanding of Him came the connection, joy, and relationship with the person of the Holy Spirit. And then the overflow of His love and my prayer language.* **Pneuma Life** *leads a reader to a time of connection with the Holy Spirit. During this time, healing happens and then a breakthrough—His love breaks through any fears and lies and overflows as* **Pneuma Life**.

Joulia Tchembrovskaia, Esq.
Immigration Attorney
Austin, TX

Pneuma Life was the catalyst sending me on a journey freeing me from my human definition of the Holy Spirit to a biblical knowledge of Him. While attending a small group Bible study using *Pneuma Life*, I met the Holy Spirit and His fullness, and I began to experience God's Word. Instead of the Bible being merely printed words on a page, it became alive *and active within me, transforming my life. The Holy Spirit not only set me on fire with an indescribable love for Him, but to experience God's love for me and all that He offers. Each scripture-filled chapter is uniquely written to help you understand who the Holy Spirit is, His role in the Godhead, His attributes, and steps to help the reader walk in His fullness and gifts today.*

Marjorie Boutain
Registered Nurse
The Home Church, Fairfield, CA

Pneuma Life

---

*Living in the
Holy Spirit's Overflow*

Sue Boldt

Cover Photo: PublicCo - Canva

This book is dedicated to all my wonderful girls…

Dayspring, Shiloh, Dea,
Avriella, Finley, Lucy, and Penny

Contents

Introduction

I have just awakened from my usual weekly Sunday afternoon nap. I work forty hours a week for a well-known healthcare company. I also am a pastor on the staff of a thriving church where my husband is the lead pastor, and by week's end, or rather at the beginning of a week, as some would say, I am exhausted. Full-time work combined with almost full-time ministry—I consider my workplace as my second pastorate—poops me out. You can find me on Sunday afternoons after church services, lunch, and errands snoozing on my bed with my beloved dog, Heidi, napping on the floor beside me.

Today, I awake to the wind exploding through the four gigantic eucalyptus trees that stand directly behind our two-story home. They sound like a holy freight train coming through my upstairs windows. I cannot see this current of air, but I can surely notice its effects on these beautiful, God-painted trees. Today they are astir, and they dance a mighty dance. Birds are soaring effortlessly on the lifts of wind above the trees. Clouds are in a constant state of intricate sculpture and movement. On the ground, leaves and debris are flying every which way. And this, my dear one, is where *Pneuma* starts.

Introduction

I wrote these opening paragraphs almost ten years ago. Nothing has changed in my desire to see the Holy Spirit at work through my own life and the life of any hungry heart for more of God's miraculous work in their life. In fact, my hunger and the world's need for more of heaven on earth have never been greater.

Evangelist and founder of Christ for All Nations, Reinhard Bonnke, writes:

> *The Spirit is the atmosphere of heaven itself, and heaven comes down here with Him. He is...the wind of heaven, blowing through our stuffy traditions and stagnation and bringing times of refreshing on all.*[1]

The world needs more of heaven on earth.

Nevertheless, these ten years later, having led a few-thousand people in studying what God's Word has to say about the Third Person of the Trinity—the Holy Spirit—and leading close to that number in receiving His overflow or baptism, I realized this simple study needed some updating. This book is essentially the same, but with added quotes from noted authors, more recent stories, and yes, some minor doctrinal changes through greater study of the Scriptures.

So, let's continue—why *Pneuma Life?*

Pneuma is the Greek New Testament word for *Spirit.*

Pneuma Greek—Meaning: *Breath, breeze, a current of air, wind, spirit.* Compare the English: pneumonia, pneumatology, pneumatic.

Think of it!

- Think of the sweetness of a baby's breath upon your chest.
- Think of your lungs filling with the clarity of air found at a mountain retreat.

- Think of a balmy tropical breeze covering your body in comfort and warmth or cool refreshing in the midst of the heat.
- Think of a hurricane-force wind where nothing can stand in its path.
- Think of the air around you during times of seeking and reflection: still, quiet, a holy hush.

These are the descriptors of the Person of the triune God that the Bible names the *Holy Spirit*. We cannot see the Holy Spirit, but we surely can feel and sense Him and see His movement all around. Just as the wind, He cannot be caught. He cannot be grasped or manipulated. He cannot be put into a box. He most certainly is God. Co-equal, co-existent, co-eternal, and co-divine with the Father and the Son.

You will notice that this Bible study workbook might be a little different from other studies that you have done. Each chapter opens with scripture verses to read and then asks for your response in the spaces provided. Working through this portion of the study will help God's Word come alive for you personally. Following these opening chapter sections, you will find a bit of commentary and practical—in today's world—examples and experiences for you to compare with your answers and notes. If you wish, you may jump directly to these latter chapter portions simply to read them as commentary instead of completing the study questions.

Now, here's the deal. However you approach this study book (no guilt here about jumping to the commentary section!), first ask the Lord Jesus to open the eyes of your heart to see the Scriptures in ways you may never have before. Because doing this is the crucial thing about this or any Bible study. What is the Holy Spirit speaking to you about Himself from either the opening verses or those found in the commentary sections? What is He saying to you directly in this moment? You will find yourself more engaged if you approach the Bible as God's Word directly breathing His instruction, encouragement, and guidance into your current life's circumstances.

Introduction

If you are reading this as a personal study, take your time and ponder the verses and commentary of each chapter. If you are doing this as a group study, then have various people read the passages out loud, using different translations of the Bible. You will learn so much from what others have to say, and they will learn from you! Make a note of everything that *strikes a chord* or resonates with you.

To further enhance your study, you can access short, accompanying videos by searching YouTube: *Sue Boldt Pneuma Life*.

Are you ready? Let's take a deep breath and spread our heart's wings. Let's invite the Spirit of the Living God to lift us to even greater heights in Him. I remember well the glory of those eucalyptus trees outside my window so many years ago. Watching that unseen natural force make itself known through the rustling and unfurling of their limbs. And now, more than ever, I hunger to see the glory of the supernatural force of the Holy Spirit breathe His life through me, and I am assured that you desire the same thing too.

Together, let's request His extraordinary into our ordinary, His supernatural into our natural everyday footsteps and routines, spilling over into our families, workplaces, the marketplace, our churches, neighborhoods, and the nations of the world with sensitivity, soundness, practicality, and power.

Let's begin…

> *If you then being evil, know how to give good gifts to your children, How much more will your heavenly Father give the Holy Spirit to those who ask Him!*
> Luke 11:13

---

[1] Reinhard Bonnke, *Holy Spirit: Are We Flammable or Fireproof?* (Orlando, FL; Christ for All Nations, 2017) page 80.

1
Let's Begin...

We will open our exploration of the Person and work of the Holy Spirit by first looking at the Old Testament. Every page of the sixty-six books of the Bible has the Holy Spirit's breath upon them. Nevertheless, in our short study, we will look at only a few passages to garner a better understanding that the Holy Spirit truly is God.

Usually referred to as the third Person of the Trinity, the Holy Spirit is not a *second-class citizen* when it comes to God the Father and God the Son. God's Word clearly states that the three persons of the Trinity are co-equal, co-divine, co-eternal, and co-existent.

Let's examine the following Old Testament passages to glimpse the Holy Spirit in action.

In the very first verse of the Bible, we find the fascinating Hebrew word *Elohim* which is translated as *God* in our English Bibles. This plural masculine noun is so interesting because it is used over 2,500 times in the Old Testament to denote the one true God.

Elohim Hebrew—Meaning: *Ruler, judge, divine One, God.*

Read **Genesis 1:1-2, 26**. What do these passages say regarding the Spirit's participation in creating planet earth?

_____

_____

_____

The Old Testament of the Bible was written in the Hebrew language of the people of Israel, through whom God chose to display His loving and redeeming intentions for all of humanity. The definition of the Hebrew word for *Spirit,* comes as no surprise.

Ruah Hebrew—Meaning: *Wind, breath, spirit.*

Now, realizing that the New and Old Testament words for *Spirit* are translated with the same meanings (see Introduction), how does His participation in man's creation speak to you in **Genesis 2:7?**

_____

_____

_____

In **John 1:1-4, 14,** we see another account of creation. In this powerful passage, the apostle John describes the **Lord Jesus** as the Word of God. Taking the creation accounts found in Genesis and John together, what do you further learn about the beginning of humanity?

_____

_____

_____

The Holy Spirit is mentioned again in **Genesis 6:3**. Ponder the passage carefully. What touches your heart when reading this? Please elaborate in your own words:

_____

_____

Let's look at just a few Old Testament examples where the Holy Spirit is recognized among men. **Genesis 41** tells a portion of a wonderful story regarding a man named Joseph. If you are not familiar with the story, take time to read the whole chapter; otherwise, simply turn to **Genesis 41:37-41**. What does Pharaoh recognize and value in Joseph's life and share why you think that is so?

_____

_____

_____

God worked through Moses to lead the children of Israel out of captivity from Egypt, as recorded in Exodus. Their journey is a powerful story and very much a picture describing how the Lord leads us out of our own bondages and strongholds. Moses has a particularly trying time with the foolishness of the nation of Israel (also like us!). Read **Numbers 11:23-29**. What particularly touches your heart about Moses, the Spirit, and the elders of Israel?

_____

_____

_____

The Bible shares King David's beautiful but tumultuous life from his youth as a shepherd to his death as the most beloved king of Israel. He had an intimate walk with God that we all aspire to **1 Samuel 13:14, Psalm 27.**

1 Samuel 16:1-13 tells of David's receiving God's anointing as the King of Israel after King Saul loses his position due to rebellion. Turn to **verse 13**, understanding that the famous account of David and Goliath is in the following chapter. Relate your thoughts regarding this pivotal point in David's life when he receives the Holy Spirit's anointing:

_____

_____

_____

From this place of Holy Spirit anointing upon his life, King David moves on to perform numerous fantastic exploits on behalf of God and His people. David's heartfelt worship and ministry in writing exquisite psalms of his love for the Lord, the anguish and superlatives of humanity, and the coming Messiah, have comforted, encouraged, and emboldened believers through the centuries. Yet, David succumbs to sin in a time of vulnerability in the midst of his victories by committing adultery and murder.

Psalm 51 is David's heart's cry for forgiveness during this deep valley in his life. Ponder his words in verses **Psalm 51:10-13** and record what impacts your heart concerning David and his relationship with the Spirit:

_____

_____

_____

_____

The entire Old Testament speaks of judges, kings, and prophets _upon whom_ we witness the Holy Spirit working. In doing so, the Old Testament points to the day when the Messiah would come, not only to rescue Israel from her bondage but to rescue all of humankind from the effects of sin in the world brought on by the disobedience of Adam and Eve.

We'll close our look at the Old Testament with two prominent passages that relate some very real promises that signal the anointing and work of the Holy Spirit in the Savior to come. Turn to **Isaiah 61:1-7** and record every promise that you can find listed here that foretells what Jesus' ministry would be like:

- _____

- _____

- _____
- _____
- _____
- _____
- _____
- _____
- _____

Now, we will turn to one of the minor prophets in the Old Testament and read God's promises for the final days leading to the second coming of the Lord Jesus. Turn to **Joel 2:28-29**. Record the Spirit's promises here to future believers in the Messiah:

- _____
- _____
- _____
- _____
- _____

———————⊝———————

Holy Spirit Breath...

The Hebrew and Greek definitions of the word *Spirit* never cease to amaze. Should we try to put God in a box of our own design, thinking that we have Him all figured out, the mere definition of *Spirit* reveals that we will never comprehend even a mere thimbleful of Who He is. As stated earlier, just like a breath, a breeze, or the wind that we cannot actually see but is blowing all around us, we can experience the Spirit's movement and see His effect on everything He touches.

Considering that the words *Ruah* or *Pneuma* both mean *breath, air, wind, or spirit,* we are reminded that breath and the ability to breathe are the sustenance of all life.

And the Lord God formed man of the dust of the ground, and breathed into his nostrils the breath of life; and man became a living being.
Genesis 2:7

God's Holy breath dwells within us.

What a stunning account of the Spirit of God being the very breath that brought man, formed from dust, into a living being. God was sharing His same life breath with His beloved creation. And, if breath is life itself, how much more the Holy Spirit, as His holy breath within us, a treasure beyond compare?

The Holy Spirit *does not ever* depart from us as born-again in the Spirit believers; nevertheless, we can quench or hinder His working **1 Thessalonians 5:19**. Our attitudes, selfishness, and sin, to put it bluntly, can cause us to not realize or experience His presence in our midst, even though the Biblical truth remains that He is always present!

I once considered *dry seasons* when I didn't experience the Lord's felt presence in my walk with Him were due to difficult circumstances or that these were just a normal part of a believer's life. However, God's Word and personal experience tell me otherwise. The Lord doesn't ever intend for His children to sense any barrenness of His *felt* love through the Holy Spirit. Indeed, He desires the polar opposite **John 15:9, Romans 5:5**.

When facing challenges or when we are in the throes of everyday life, the Holy Spirit confirms to us His love, peace, joy, and power experientially. Again, our sense of *feeling* like we are in a spiritual desert may be the direct result of our walking in other directions from Him that are not helpful or that we simply haven't taken the time to be alone with Him to cultivate His presence.

The Holy Spirit was present at the very start of creation. **Isaiah 40:12-14** and **Psalm 104:30** also remind us of this truth. The three Persons of the Godhead each had a part to play in creating humanity and the world. We see this in the wording of **Genesis 1:26**, *Let us...*

- God the Father, the Master Designer, spoke His Word **Genesis 1:3.**
- The Word was Jesus **John 1:14**.
- The Spirit breathed life into what was created. He brought what was *void* or worthless and made sense of it all, giving it value and purpose **Genesis 2:7**.

Pastor and theologian, Dr. Steve Schell, writes:

> *Because there is perfect unity between the Father, Son, and Holy Spirit, there is no difference between them in will, capacity, or character...*
>
> *Scripture shows that within this One, whom we call God, there is a community of three persons: Father, Son, and Holy Spirit who are one in nature and one in purpose.[1]*

Holy Spirit and Us...

In **Genesis 1:2**, we find that before God created earth and humanity as we know them, *the earth was without form, and **void**; and darkness was on the face of the deep...*

Let's look at the word translated as *void* in the prior sentence and verse:

Tohu Hebrew—Meaning: *A formless, chaotic mess, a waste, a worthless thing, emptiness, and desolation, for no purpose, and for nothing.*

That sure sounds like my life before I became a Christian. Indeed, it sounds like my life now at times when I stray from Him, and I try to live life without the direction of the Holy Spirit **Galatians 3:1-5**. When I am in that self-determined state, I experience much confusion and chaos. The apostle Paul in the New Testament wrote to the church in Corinth that *God is not the author of confusion but of peace.* **1 Corinthians 14:33.**

In **Genesis 6:3**, we learn that the Spirit won't contend or strive with men forever. Though He is constantly pursuing, wooing, striving, and contending for our best and highest good, there may be times when He stands back and lets us *have our own way.* This attribute reflects the Holy Spirit's personality. He is a gentleman, not forcing His way where He is not invited. Knowing this about Him is food for thought. In other words, if we want to be in control of an area of our lives or situations we face, He won't be!

In the Old Testament, we read that the Holy Spirit more often came *upon* a person rather than residing *in* them, as the New Testament so clearly states takes place in the life of a Christian. The Spirit was *upon* people to perform supernatural tasks, lead and speak to the nations, and even create beautiful works of art and architecture that glorified God. This is the unique difference between life before Jesus came and the life of His followers now.

Recall Moses' comment that he wished all the elders of Israel had the Spirit upon them. And when they did experience His presence, it was a one-time incident **Numbers 11:25**. Jesus states in **Luke 10:23-24** that the Old Testament prophets and kings longed to participate in what we now experience, see, and understand.

Our Spirit and Soul...

David's cry for forgiveness from the Lord found in **Psalm 51** eloquently expresses our hearts when we have stumbled and fallen into sin. The psalm is beautiful poetry, but more importantly, it describes the depth of an intimate relationship between a person and their beloved Father.

> *Create in me a clean heart O God,*
> *And renew a steadfast spirit within me.*
> *Do not cast me away from Your presence*
> *And do not take Your Holy Spirit from me.*
> **Psalm 51:10-11**

Let's take a look at two essential thoughts from this passage. The first is the Bible's distinction between our spirit and soul—seen as our *heart* in the verse above. Although we are examining the Old Testament here, we will cross over briefly into the New Testament to gain a bit more clarity.

> *Now may the God of peace Himself sanctify you completely; and may your whole **spirit, soul,** and **body** be preserved blameless at the coming of our Lord Jesus Christ.*
> **1 Thessalonians 5:23**

Like Him, we are tri-part beings.

God created us in His image **Genesis 1:26,** and we, like Him, are tri-part beings. God is *Father, Son,* and *Holy Spirit,* and we have a *body, soul,* and *spirit.* We get that we have a body! Yet, the difference between our *soul* and *spirit* can be confusing.

Our hearts and emotions, minds and thought-life, personality, ability to choose, and intellect all fall into the arena of our soul. Let's consider both the Hebrew and Greek words used that our translated as *soul* in our Bibles:

Nephesh Hebrew—Meaning: *Soul, a life, a living being, self, person, mind, personality, inner desires, and feelings.* The word occurs more than 750 times in the Old Testament. *Soul* is the word usually chosen in translations for *nephesh,* but heart, person, life, and mind are also used when best suited. *Nephesh* can also describe the whole person: spirit, soul, and body.

Psyche or Psuche or Greek—Meaning: *The immaterial part of a person's being including the features of self-consciousness, will, reason, and conscience.* It is specifically the seat of a person's *emotions, thoughts, thought processes, the ability to choose, will, desires, understanding, affections, passions, and intellect.* Simply, *the soul is the place of the heart and mind of a person and what we would term their personality. The soul is that which strictly belongs to the person himself.*

Born Again...

We not only consist of a body and soul; the Lord created us with a *spirit.* The same words *ruah* and *pneuma* are used for our spirit and the Holy Spirit in the Old and New Testaments. Our *spirit* is where we have communion with God.

When Adam and Eve chose to turn from God in the garden of Eden, death came upon them just as God had warned them **Genesis 2:17**. Not only did their physical bodies begin the aging and death process, but their spirit died instantly, resulting in their separation from God. That sweet place of relationship with Him experienced death eternally, and the Apostle Paul declares that these consequences for their sin were passed onto us **Romans 5:12-16**.

We must receive spiritual CPR.

Now, we can understand why Jesus said that we must be *born again* of the Spirit **John 3:5-8**. We may have been born physically, but our *spirit* needs to be *born again* with the life breath of the Holy Spirit. And this is precisely what happens when an individual receives the Lord into their life by faith **John 1:12**. The very breath of God breathes life into their spirit, reinstating eternal life with Him. Literally, spiritual CPR! This act of the Holy Spirit is reminiscent of

His breath pouring into Adam at the time of creation, restoring us to the high honor of being called a child of God.

Paul, in **Ephesians 2:5-6**, states:

> ...*even when we were dead in our trespasses, (He) made us alive together with Christ.*

In simple terms, our spirit communes with and knows God in a personal relationship. Our soul is who we are: unique, unlike anyone else, with our distinct personalities, thoughts, desires, will, and intellect. God so loved us that He gave His Son to restore both our spirit and soul to Himself.[2] Our bodies are our temporary *tent* that holds the whole enchilada together. Truly, we are *fearfully and wonderfully made!* **Psalm 139:14**.

The second distinction made in **Psalm 51** is that knowing or experiencing God's presence is equated with the Holy Spirit. David knew that having the Holy Spirit depart from him meant that God's very presence was leaving.

As believers, we need to understand that the Holy Spirit makes the Godhead known and experienced **John 16:14-15**. Like David and many others in the Old Testament who enjoyed God's discernable presence, the folks we read about in the New Testament also tangibly knew the power of the Holy Spirit. They experienced overwhelming *joy and power* on the Day of Pentecost **Acts 2:12-13**. We learn that Paul felt *peace that passes understanding* **Philippians 4:7** and the *love* and *joy* of the Holy Spirit **Romans 5:5, 14:17**. The Spirit's presence was genuine and authentic to the New Testament believers and can now be known by us.

Rev. Dennis Bennett, the late Episcopal priest and seminal figure in the Holy Spirit charismatic renewal of the 1970's, wrote:

> *The new life created by the Holy Spirit in us, is what Jesus calls "eternal life." This doesn't just mean "going on and*

*on," but God's life in us, the kind of life that never runs down, never gets tired or bored, but is always joyful and fresh **1 John 5:11.**[3]*

Holy Spirit and the Prophets...

Scholars agree that **Isaiah 61:1-7** is a prophetic description of the coming Messiah written approximately 700 years before Christ walked the earth. These verses exquisitely depict the future ministry of the Lord Jesus in the power of the Holy Spirit as we read about it in the four gospel accounts. Jesus validates His ministry by quoting from this passage that He is the fulfillment of Isaiah's prophecy in **Luke 4:17-21**. Isaiah's prophetic word also foretold what His church—each one of us—would *continue* doing in the same power of the Holy Spirit's anointing. These promises speak to us of God's absolute love and ability towards us to heal, save, and deliver.

The prophet Joel spoke about the day we now live when the Holy Spirit is pouring out upon all who name Jesus Christ as Lord **Joel 2:21-29**. God's Spirit is no longer being relegated to just a few key people, as in the Old Testament, but has come upon and dwells within *all* believers—men and women, young and old. Joel foretold the mighty works of the Holy Spirit by signs and wonders, and His enabling God's servants to prophesy, see visions, and dream great dreams. Peter quotes Joel on the day of Pentecost as the fulfillment of this Old Testament promise, ushering in the new church age in the Spirit **Acts 2:16-21**.

Now, let's look forward in our Bibles to see what we can learn about the Holy Spirit from the words of the Lord Jesus Himself and those who experienced the Holy Spirit in the New Testament.

I hope you are as excited as I am to examine further what God's Word says about the Holy Spirit!

---

[1] Dr. Steve Schell, *The Promise of the Father: Understanding and Receiving the Baptism with the Holy Spirit* (Federal Way, Washington; Life Lessons Publishing, 2020), page 21.

[2] For a Biblical study regarding restoring our souls from life's hurts and lies from the enemy, consider reading *Refresh: Transformed Thoughts, Emotions and Lives*, by Sue Boldt. Available on Amazon.

[3] Rev. Dennis and Rita Bennett, *The Holy Spirit and You: A Study-Guide to the Spirit-Filled Life* (Plainfield, NJ; Logos International, 1971), page 14.

Study Questions:

- What spoke to you most from this chapter?

- How does knowing that the Biblical words for *spirit* mean breath or breeze speak to your heart?

- Looking back at the bullet points on *page 7*, share your thoughts about the unity, harmony, love, and action between the Father, Son, and Holy Spirit.

- Put into your own words what it means to be *born again of the Spirit.*

- God's Word tells us that He wants us to not only know Him intellectually with our minds but for us also to experience His love, joy, peace, and power. How does this encourage you?

2

The Spirit

and

The Savior

We covered ground in the Old Testament by viewing the Holy Spirit's relationship to the Godhead and His tremendous influence upon humanity. Now, we will follow the Lord Jesus in His ministry in the Spirit upon the earth. Take some quiet moments and ask the Lord to give you fresh eyes to see truths out of His Word that maybe you haven't noticed before. As Paul would say, *that the eyes of your understanding would be enlightened* **Ephesians 1:18**. It will be worth it!

The Messiah, though wholly God, was made flesh to become the sinless sacrifice that would restore man's relationship with the Father. What do we find out about Jesus in **Philippians 2:5-8** and **Hebrews 2:14-18**?

_____

_____

_____

Each of the Gospels gives an account of Jesus' water baptism by John the Baptist in **Matthew 3:16-17, Mark 1:9-11, Luke 3:21-22, John 1:32-34.** Read one or all of these accounts and think about what took place. Do these words have implications for us? Share your thoughts:

_____

_____

_____

All four New Testament Gospel writers also record a statement made by John the Baptist that must be important because they each share the same message. Please turn to one or all of the passages and explain what you think John means by using the phrases *baptism in the Spirit and by fire*. **Matthew 3:11-12, Mark 1:7-8, Luke 3:16, John 1:32-34**:

_____

_____

_____

Following Jesus' water baptism and the descent of the Holy Spirit upon Him, the Spirit then leads Him to confront and overcome Satan in the wilderness **Matthew 4:1-11, Mark 1:12-13, Luke 4:1-13**. Jesus resists the temptations of the enemy and turns them on their heads! **Hebrews 4:14-16**. Turn to **Luke 4:14-21** to read what Jesus does immediately following the temptation encounter. You will recognize some of these verses from the previous chapter. What speaks to your heart?

_____

_____

_____

We read that Jesus, God incarnate, is totally dependent on the Father and the working of the Holy Spirit. Read **John 5:16-20** and **John 14:7-11**. What does Jesus say about Himself here?

_____

_____

_____

Jesus, the Messiah, lived a life like no other. It is vital for us to view how He lived His life so that we might learn from His example for our own walk with God. Listed are passages *where* we continually find our Lord Jesus. Take a moment to look up a few or all of them **Matthew 14:22-23, Mark 6:45-46, Luke 5:16.** What do they say about the Lord, and how can we apply His actions to our lives?

_____

_____

_____

To close the study portion of this chapter, turn to **John 3:6-8**. There, a ruler of the Jews visits Jesus under the cover of darkness. Nicodemus truly seeks the source of power for Jesus' miraculous ministry. He also hungers for a relationship with God. In answer to Nicodemus' questions, Jesus instructs him that he must be born again of the Spirit. When reading this passage, what thoughts come to your mind regarding the Hebrew and Greek meaning of the word *Spirit?*

_____

_____

_____

———————————$\mathcal{S}$———————————

Lavish Grace and Holy Spirit Power...

I hope you are sensing an excitement about Who the Holy Spirit is, His work in the world, and in you as an individual. It is thrilling to realize that the God of the universe would pursue each of us to live eternally with Him. Even more, He extends to us a personal invitation for a close and intimate relationship with Him. On this side of heaven, we will never be able to understand who God is fully and the magnitude of His love for the likes of us!

Jesus,

God's plan

for our rescue.

It is almost incomprehensible that God took on human form and dwelt among us. One of Jesus' titles, *Immanuel*, literally means *God with us*. Not only did God come to planet earth, but He became like us—*He took off His God robes* and put on flesh **Philippians 2:6-7, Hebrews 2:17**. He had to. It was God's plan of redemption and rescue for His lost creation that only a perfect, spotless, sinless human could pay the ultimate ransom price by shedding His blood **Leviticus 17:11, 1 Corinthians 5:7**.

When Adam and Eve disobeyed God's word in the Garden, thereby ushering in evil, they not only threw every human after them *under the bus* because of their sin, but they also aligned themselves with God's adversary, the devil. Adam and Eve opened the door for disease, disaster, disorder, and death to enter the glorious, breathtaking world God had made for His beloved creation **Romans 5:12-21**. Since that time, the human race has been held captive by the evil one because of missing the mark of God's perfection. Subsequently, our own sin has held us captive to the enemy and evil, as well.

Because our sin caused the entrance of death upon our lives, Jesus took the death penalty for us so that we might live. What the blood of animals could not accomplish, the Savior's precious blood did once and for all **Hebrews 10:10**. Because we find the life of all flesh in its blood, God required a blood sacrifice for the atonement of *sin* **Leviticus 17:11**. When Jesus cried from the cross, *It is finished,* He meant it! **John 19:30**. He declared His finished work for our ransom from captivity and death and reinstated our eternal destiny with Him. And as if that were not enough, Jesus' sacrifice also procured our authority over the devil in the power of His name and Word **Colossians 2:13-15, Luke 10:17-20**.

Author, professor, and speaker, Maureen Broderson, states this regarding our authority in spiritual warfare prayer:

In this battle against the realms of darkness, we realize victory only as we bring the enemy to the ultimate place of true judgment: The Cross. We drive the adversary to Calvary. Herein we see the essence of prayerful spiritual warfare—to bring every issue generated by sin, self, or Satan and all his cohorts, to the place where the blood of Jesus Christ spilled, the place where the forces of darkness were, and forever will be defeated. You'll find this to be true in your personal life or as you pray for the nations of the world.[1]

Our restored relationship with God is based purely upon His lavish grace—not our works or good efforts. His resurrection *sealed the deal* by demonstrating His authority over the prince of death, the devil **Hebrews 2:14-15**. As **Ephesians 4:8** states, *He led captivity captive*—setting us free! How amazing is the wondrous love of God that He moved heaven and earth to bring us back to His embrace!

We can never say to Him, *You don't understand what I'm going through!* Oh yes, He understands! He experienced *every* type of temptation, *every* wound imaginable, and *every* human emotion because He became like us, clay and dust—wholly human. Yet, He never faltered in relying entirely upon the Father and the Holy Spirit as He walked the earth.

Why is our understanding this about Jesus so essential to our study of the Holy Spirit? Because we realize that when Jesus gave up the riches of heaven and limited Himself to a finite body, He became just as dependent upon the Holy Spirit as we are now.

*For you know the grace of our Lord Jesus Christ, that though **He** was rich, yet for your sakes **He became poor**, that you through His poverty might become rich.*
2 Corinthians 8:9 (emphasis added)

Jesus shows us the way of complete and total dependence upon the Father by listening intently for His voice and by ministering and living only in the power of the Holy Spirit. The Triune God works in perfect harmony and glory.

Dove and Fire...

It must be essential that we note that the Holy Spirit came upon the Lord Jesus after His water baptism because the event is recorded in all four Gospels. Again, we see the Trinity in action, but even more, we note that the anointing of the Spirit was necessary for Jesus to begin His earthly, miraculous ministry. This coming-upon of the Holy Spirit has significant implications for us as well.

The Holy Spirit taking the form of a dove possibly denotes the gentle side of the Spirit's character. Consider how easily they fly away where there is commotion or agitation. The Bible tells us not to grieve the Holy Spirit and lists some ways we can allow this to happen **Ephesians 4:30-32**. I remember times when sensing His presence only to have it diminish when I've been careless in my words or actions. The world has long used doves as a symbol of peace taken from Noah's account of God's wrath receding from the earth as the floodwaters receded **Genesis 8:10-11**.

Holy Spirit anointing, needed for the miraculous.

When writing about the Holy Spirit's movement within a corporate gathering of believers, Paul reaffirms this truth about the gentle nature of the Holy Spirit at work:

> *For God is not the author of confusion but of peace...*
> **1 Corinthians 14:33**

On the other end of the spectrum of the Spirit's personality or character is His comparison with *fire*. John the Baptist prophecies, as all four Gospel writers account, that Jesus would baptize believers with the Holy Spirit and with fire. For now, let's consider the second half of this phrase with fire—we will look at the phrase *baptism in the Spirit* in a coming chapter:

I indeed baptize you with water unto repentance,
But He who is coming after me is mightier than I,
Whose sandals I am not worth to carry.
He will baptize you with the Holy Spirit and fire.
Matthew 3:11

The explanation for the term *fire* is given in the following verse:

His winnowing fan is in His hand,
And He will thoroughly clean out His threshing floor,
And gather His wheat into the barn;
But he will burn up the chaff with unquenchable fire.
Matthew 3:12

Fire both purifies and destroys. It also brings warmth and comfort. It also can spread rapidly, changing the composition of any and everything it touches.

Holy Spirit fire purifies us.

The Holy Spirit's work in a person's life is often like fire. The warmth of His character comforts us in our times of need. He also purifies our unhealthy and harmful behaviors, burning the strongholds of the enemy in our lives that keep us from fully experiencing all God has for us. The Spirit initially draws us to Jesus, setting the fire in motion, working in us all of the days of our earthly lives to change the composition of our hearts and minds into the image of Christ as we surrender to Him. The fire of the Spirit is the power of the gospel on display, healing lives and bodies and softening and warming the coldest heart.

On the day of Pentecost, the disciples saw what appeared to be tongues of fire on each of their heads as the Spirit was lavishly poured out upon them. Those gathered also heard the sound of a mighty rushing wind. The Holy Spirit was demonstrating the intensity, passion, and pursuing power of the gospel that would be preached to the uttermost parts of the earth as Jesus said it would be.

In the Midst of Temptation...

God's Word states that after the Spirit came upon our Lord Jesus, He led Jesus into the wilderness to confront the devil. We cannot comprehend the intensity of this trial of temptation at the outset of Jesus' ministry. Jesus experienced temptation in three major categories of all seduction to sin by the devil as listed in **1 John 2:16**:

The lust of the flesh – Our attempt to use everything, every way, and by every means to satisfy our beautifully God-designed human desires (material, sexual, intellectual, and emotional) with anything other than God or His best for us. *Lust* means never being satisfied, and it also speaks of satisfaction only for our pleasure without regard for others.

The lust of the eyes – Our eyes are the gateway to our minds. What our minds dwell on directs the course of our actions. Lust is sparked by what the eye sees **Matthew 5:29, Psalm 101:3.**

The pride of life – Pride is the reason why God cast the beautiful angelic being, Lucifer, out of heaven. The enemy's pride in believing He was like God, superior to God, and pride in his God-given beauty and talents are also the exact source of much ruin in our lives **Ezekiel 28:17.** Congruently, *shame* is the flip side of *pride* that the enemy uses to ensnare human lives into living in less than God's perfect love for them.

We can see that most of our temptations stem from one or a combination of the three categories listed above. Jesus was tempted by everything that we could ever possibly be enticed with, yet He did so without giving into these entanglements **Hebrews 4:15**. It is helpful to remember that temptation in itself *is not sin*. Instead, what we *do* with temptation is what is crucial. Lingering in temptation or making room for it tips the scales against us. James concisely presents us with the process of the inception of a temptation to the full conception of sin:

> *But each one is tempted when he is drawn away by his own desires and enticed.*
>
> *Then, when desire has conceived, it gives birth to sin; and sin, when it is full-grown, brings forth death.*
>
> *Do not be deceived, my beloved brethren.*
> **James 1:14-16**

With the Holy Spirit's anointing and the authority of God's Word, Jesus was victorious in the battle in the wilderness. He understands *everything* about us and everything we face, small or large, and by His Spirit, He can supply all that we need to overcome the adversary's advances towards us **Hebrews 4:14-16.**

We also have the promise that God will not allow the enemy to entice us beyond what we can handle:

> *No temptation has overtaken you except such as is common to man; but God is faithful, who will not allow you to be tempted beyond what you are able, but with the temptation will also make the way of escape, that you may be able to bear it.*
> **1 Corinthians 10:13**

This incredible promise has brought me through to safe harbor as I've clung to the Lord in times of fierce temptation. Over and over again, the Lord has provided a way of escape. Unfortunately, too many times, I didn't choose His way out. However, that does not negate the truth of this verse and the promise of the Holy Spirit's power and grace in never ceasing His purifying work in my life or relentlessly pursuing my full rescue.

23

Dynamis Power...

Luke shares what immediately happened after the Lord's time of temptation in the wilderness:

> *Then Jesus returned in the power of the Spirit to Galilee, and news of Him went out through all the surrounding region.*
> **Luke 4:14**

By what power did Jesus initiate His miraculous earthly ministry? It was the *power* of the Holy Spirit.

Let's look at the New Testament definition of the Greek word used here for ***power***.

Jesus ministered with dynamis in the Spirit.

Dynamis Greek—Meaning: *Energy, power, might, great force, extraordinary ability, and strength.* Compare this word with *dynamic* or *dynamite* in English. All the words derived from the stem *Dyna-* have the meaning of *being able and capable.* The *power for performing miracles.* It also means *moral power and excellence of soul. To be able.*

The amount, depth, and scope of Jesus' miracles set Him apart from any other god that the world has tried to conjure up. He truly is the One and Only **John 1:14 NIV**. But now, we see that He did these mighty workings in the power or *dynamis* of the Spirit. He needed the Spirit then while walking the earth, as we do now in our earthly sojourn.

How did Jesus, after choosing to set aside His Godly prerogatives as he walked the dusty roads of Palestine and live as one of us, sustain the *dynamis* of the Spirit? He said that He only did those things which He saw the Father doing **John 5:16-20, John 14:7-11**. He didn't say or do anything other than what the Father directed Him to do in the power of the Spirit.

Guy Duffield and Nathaniel Van Cleave write:

> *Jesus was indeed very God, but when He came into this world*
> *it seems that He subjected Himself to the Father in such a way*
> *that His ministry was through the direction and power of the*
> *Holy Spirit...His preaching, healing, casting out devils, and*
> *even in His death and resurrection.*[2]

In the gospels, we often read that Jesus went somewhere alone to spend time with the Father **Matthew 14:23, Mark 1:35, Luke 6:12**. Knowing this is vital for solving the question asked above. Although the crowds were pressing, humanity's need was overwhelming, and the activities of His life were incomprehensibly demanding—Jesus always devoted time alone with God.

Knowing about Jesus' intimacy with the Father is crucial for our walk with Him in the power of the Holy Spirit. Our Lord Jesus didn't let anything, even good and wonderful things, deter Him from spending precious time with His Father in sweet fellowship and renewal.

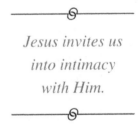

Jesus invites us into intimacy with Him.

Jesus also invites us to a similar communion with Himself and our Father **Matthew 6:6, John 15:9, Revelation 3:20**. This invitation is one of the extravagant gifts of the gospel: the invitation to have an intimate and personal relationship with God Himself. And it is the Holy Spirit who makes these precious times practical, authentic, and experienced in our spirit, affecting our soul and body **John 16:13-15, Romans 8:14-17**.

From my own book, *Refresh: Transformed Thoughts, Emotions and Lives...*

> *Cultivating God's presence in our lives is a feast for our souls*
> *and spirits.*[3] *The lusts and cravings of this world seem*
> *valueless when we invite the Holy Spirit to overflow and*

overwhelm us.[4] By experiencing times of refreshing in the presence of the Lord, old lies that once held us become less tempting to return to because of the beauty of His presence. Ministry burnout is less likely to take place because we are ministering out of His fullness in our lives rather than ministering on the empty fumes of our own strength.[5]

Everything we long for can be found in God alone.

What do you need today? Guidance, freedom, satisfaction, deliverance from the enemy, material or physical needs met, healing? Whatever you need or could ever desire can be found in Him. Jesus, while in His humanity, knew the Source of all fulfillment. Couldn't we follow in His footsteps and meet the Lord in our own *secret place* to hear His voice and receive daily direction for our lives and ministry?

> *But you, when you pray, go into your room, and when you have shut your door, pray to your Father who is in the **secret place**; and your Father who sees in secret will reward you openly.*
> **Matthew 6:6.** (emphasis, mine)

We come to the close of this chapter by looking at Jesus' words to Nicodemus in *John 3:1-8*, reaffirming what the Holy Spirit is like:

> *The wind blows where it wishes, and you hear the sound of it, but cannot tell where it comes from and where it goes. So is everyone who is born of the Spirit.*
> **John 3:8**

The wind. There is that description and definition again. The Spirit can be soft and gentle like a summer breeze to bring refreshment to the weary; or strong and mighty with the force of a hurricane to tear down any edifice that the enemy or our flesh has built up. He can breathe a whisper into our lives or stir things up like a tornado. He cannot be captured or trivialized, bought or sold, put on the shelf, or forgotten. He is the very breath of God, and He is God. He woos the wretched sinner to the embrace of the Father and Son and relentlessly works within them all the days of their lives to walk in all the blessing, presence, inheritance, gifts, and fruit of the Lord Jesus.

Isn't the Holy Spirit extraordinary? We close this chapter with the heartfelt lyrics from a worship song inviting the Holy Spirit in greater measure into our lives. The lyrics simply state…

Fire and wind, come and do it again
Open up the gates, let Heaven on in.
Come rest on us.
Come rest on us.
So come down
Spirit, when You move You make my heart pound
When You fill the room.
You're here and I know You are moving
I'm here and I know You will fill me.[6]

---

[1] Maureen Broderson, *Victorious Spiritual Warfare, So Simple, Grandma Can Do It* (Washington D.C.; Vide Press, 2021), pages 69-70.

[2] Guy P. Duffield and Nathaniel M. Van Cleave, *Foundations of Pentecostal Theology* (Los Angeles, CA; Foursquare Media, 2008), pages 279-280.

[3] Psalm 16:11, Psalm 36:8, Isaiah 55:2, Jeremiah 31:14

[4] Romans 5:5

[5] Sue Boldt, *Refresh: Transformed Thoughts, Emotions, and Lives* (Las Vegas, NV, KDP Publishing, Updated 2021), page 155.

[6] *Rest on Us,* Antoine Brown, Brandon Lake, Elyssa Smith, Harvest Parker, Jonathan Jay, Rebekah Erin White; January 2021

Study Questions:

- What spoke to you most from this chapter?

- Have you experienced the Holy Spirit working in your life in the manner of a dove or as fire? Share one of these seasons.

- Looking back at the categories of temptation we face on *page 22*, think about your own life. Did the Holy Spirit illuminate any particular one of these categories where you find yourself more vulnerable?

- Share what Holy Spirit *dynamis* means to your life and ministry.

- How does Jesus' example of spending time in intimacy with the Father speak to your heart regarding His miraculous ministry or for your own life?

3

The Beloved's Record

The Gospel of John records Jesus' vivid descriptions of the Holy Spirit's work in more detail than the other three books about Jesus' life.

Jesus nicknamed John and his brother, James, the *sons of thunder*. Both men were radically transformed by the limitless and lavish love of Christ **Mark 3:17**. So great was the transformation of John's life and heart by the Lord Jesus that John himself would change his calling card from a *son of thunder* to the *disciple whom Jesus loved* **John 21:7**. James would later become one of the first martyrs of the Christian faith.

In **John 14, 15,** and **16,** we find an excellent discourse on the Holy Spirit. There are unfathomable riches to be found here. However, because we are looking mainly at the working of the Holy Spirit, we will look only at small portions speaking directly about Him. Nevertheless, I encourage you to read all three chapters entirely to enhance your study of the Holy Spirit in the context in which John recorded Jesus' words.

Let's begin this chapter by asking the Lord to open the eyes of our understanding. Then let's write what is speaking to our hearts and minds regarding the Holy Spirit after each brief look of study in the spaces provided.

The first passage we'll look at is **John 14:12-18.** It follows hot on the heels of scripture that we considered in the previous chapter. Here, Jesus makes many profound statements. Write down these statements in the lines below. A few extra lines are provided, so don't be concerned about filling in each point.

- _____

- _____

- _____

- _____

- _____

- _____

- _____

- _____

- _____

Taking the next portion of verses found in **John 14:19-26,** Jesus relates more about His relationship with the Father, and He also speaks promises to us as believers. Answer these two questions:

- What moves your heart regarding the intimacy the Father and Son want to have with you?

_____

_____

- Who does Jesus say will be coming to our aid **verse 26?**

_____

Share what is meaningful to you about the *name* Jesus gives the Holy Spirit in **John 14:26,** which is also mentioned in **John 14:16.**

_____

_____

Jesus speaks again of the Holy Spirit in **John 15:26-27**. What do His words here have in common with what we just read in **John 14:19-26**? What can we deduce from the two passages?

_____

_____

_____

We will address **John 16:5-8** in sections. What does Jesus say would be advantageous or beneficial to believers upon completing His earthly ministry, and why is this important?

_____

_____

Looking at **John 15:8**, what do you think Jesus means when He states that the Holy Spirit will:

- Convict or convince the world of sin?

_____

_____

_____

- Convict or convince the world of righteousness?

_____

_____

_____

- Convict, or convince the world of judgment?

_____

_____

_____

Now read **John 16:9-11** for Jesus' explanation of the Spirit's *convincing* work. Do His words enhance your understanding of **verse 5**? If so, share further what you think Jesus is saying in the statements below regarding the Holy Spirit's work:

• Convict or convince the world of sin:

_____

_____

• Convict or convince the world of righteousness:

_____

_____

• Convict or convince the world of judgment:

_____

_____

In **John 16:12-15**, we find another set of amazing verses that I don't think we'll ever fully grasp in our minds this side of heaven. Jesus even states in **verse 12** that the disciples couldn't bear or understand everything that He was saying. Yet, here we find promises from the Lord given to every believer who has a heart to hear and to receive. Please read the passage now and answer the questions below.

Jesus calls the Holy Spirit *the Spirit of* _____. Why is that significant?

_____

_____

_____

In **verse 13**, Jesus makes an astounding statement, *He (the Spirit) will guide you into _____ truth.* Take some time to contemplate this passage and record what implications this has for your life:

_____

_____

_____

In **verses 13-15**, we again see the communion of the Godhead—Father, Son, and Spirit. In these verses, we find promises from Jesus that His Spirit will do for a believer. Share them here:

- _____

- _____

- _____

- _____

- _____

Which one of the above promises does He repeat twice for added emphasis? *He must really want us to know this particular promise!*

_____

_____

————— ⑨ —————

Holy Spirit Advantage...

As we read **John 14, 15**, and **16**, we discover much to think and pray about regarding the Person and work of the Holy Spirit. Our finite minds can only comprehend a drop of the immense, eternal ocean of who the Holy Spirit is. He cannot be tamed, put in a box, fixed to a formula, or adequately described.

It is difficult when reading **John 14:12** to adequately comprehend what Jesus meant when He stated that we, as believers in Him, would do *greater works* than He did. However, the disciples listening may have understood. Remember, they were eyewitnesses to His miracles recorded in the gospels and countless other wonders not written about **John 21:25**. Nevertheless, they had a taste of what the *greater works* might be.

At least twice, Jesus sent out groups of either twelve or seventy disciples two by two, giving them the authority and *dynamis* to accomplish miracles **Matthew 10:1-8, Mark 6:7-13, Luke 10:1-9**. His sending these disciples as representatives of His Kingdom created the potential for *more* of God's miraculous events

Let's live in Holy Spirit advantage.

to occur because a more significant number of people were ministering in His name. The miracles they experienced weren't necessarily more extraordinary in scope but greater in number.

The same holds true for us. For *our advantage* and to *advance* God's Kingdom, we must invite the Holy Spirit to have full sway over our lives so that we might see the miraculous God's Word promises us in **Mark 16:15-18**. We will discuss this further in future chapters.

Author and speaker Joyce Meyer shares this from **Ephesians 6:10** regarding our being **strong** *in the Lord:*

> *To be "in Christ" means that we believe in Him, but it also means that we do everything in our life with and for Him. Our strength comes from that kind of relationship...We need to realize that we can do nothing without Him **John 15:5**...*
>
> *God has made supernatural power available to us. The word strong is taken from a compound of two Greek words, **en** and **dynamis,** making **endynamoo**. We get our English word dynamite from the **dynamis,** because it means "explosive*

strength, ability, or power." The two words put together convey the idea of being infused or filled with this amazing power. Not only do we have this power, but the authority to use it.[1]

So, why don't we always see the miraculous take place in our western culture with the intensity and magnitude that we hear about in other parts of the world? I have personally experienced several physical healings, including a miraculous and documented physical healing from stage 4 terminal cancer. I also know God's delivering power from demonic oppression in my own life and that of many others, but I still long to see more.

Perhaps our lack of consistently seeing God's miraculous is our tendency to simply not take the time to *wait* upon the Lord to hear His direction. In our hyper-fast culture, slowing down, waiting on God, and being quiet enough to hear a word of guidance from the Holy Spirit is difficult for us to do.

Who or what are we relying upon?

Also, upon who or what are we relying? In God's effusive and generous love, the Lord has given scientists and researchers revelation of how He made things and how they work. Yes, science and the miraculous come directly from our Father in whom there is no shadow **James 1:17**. Nevertheless, who are we ultimately trusting? Are we rushing ahead of the Lord in making decisions about areas of our lives without consulting Him first?

And finally, one last possible hindrance to seeing more of the miraculous is our human nature tendency for celebrity and fame, especially in our social media culture. Could our personal motives get in the way of the Holy Spirit's touch?

Still, God's Word is true, and Lord Jesus has never changed **Hebrews 13:8**. What we read in the Books of Acts regarding the disciples continuing the dynamic and miraculous ministry of Jesus *is* possible today. The opening verse of this book states clearly that the Lord *began* His work— then Acts continues forward after Jesus' resurrection, filled with stories of the first-century church in the anointing of the Holy Spirit carrying the ball forward.

We, too, are called to seek God for the same demonstrations of His power in our generation. There are just too many Scripture passages in both the Old and New Testaments proclaiming that God's miraculous power has not been silenced through the ages. He is still God!

> *Jesus Christ is the same yesterday, today, and forever.*
> **Hebrews 12:13**

In John's Gospel, Jesus refers to the Holy Spirit as the *Helper* or *Comforter*...

Parakletos Greek—Meaning: From *para*, beside, and *kaleo*, to call. *One who is called or summoned to one's side, especially to one's aid. A helper, assistant, advocate, intercessor, comforter, and counselor.*

Jesus promises His disciples that they will never be without the aid, comfort, counsel, and power of the Holy Spirit in their lives. Does this particular name of the Spirit encourage you at this moment? We are never alone in living our lives on this planet without the absolute promise of God that His Spirit is always with us to give us strength and wisdom for every situation we will ever face.

In **John 16:7-11**, Jesus promises His disciples He will send the Holy Spirit to them after His departure. The Holy Spirit will **convict** the world of sin, righteousness, and judgment.

Let's look at these actions of the Spirit.

Conviction of Sin:

Elegcho Greek—Meaning: *To convict, convince, tell a fault, rebuke, reprove, or admonish.*

The convincing work of the Holy Spirit is an essential key for a person to acknowledge their need for redemption and come to faith in the Lord Jesus. It is the Holy Spirit who reveals to them that their sin has separated them from their Father who loves them beyond reason. Let's look at the word *sin* in the original language of the New Testament:

Hamartia Greek—Meaning: *Sin, to sin, missing the mark. Failing to meet an objective, maintain a standard, or fulfill an obligation.*

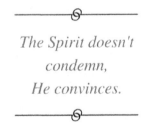

The Spirit doesn't condemn, He convinces.

Sin is simply, but devastatingly, falling short of God's glory, and dear one, we have all done that **Romans 3:23**! We have all missed the *bullseye* of God's perfection and holiness. There is not a person alive who doesn't realize their imperfection. Nevertheless, it is the Spirit's working that convinces a person that their sin is what keeps them separated from God and their need for the Savior. This convincing work of the Spirit continues throughout our lives, not just at the time of salvation.

The sweetest aspect of this challenging task that the Spirit continues in our lives is that *He doesn't condemn, He convinces* us. I don't know how He does it, but when He starts pointing out areas of my life that He longs to work on and transform, I feel remorse that I've disappointed the Lord, but I don't feel condemned. I even feel hopeful and encouraged during this convincing time because if He took the time to point it out, I have confidence that I am deeply loved, and He will come alongside me to make the change **Hebrews 12:7**.

If we are experiencing condemnation or overwhelming guilt, it is either being hurled at us by our own thoughts or the enemy, the devil. This adversary is named the *Accuser* because he is very adept at making us feel accused or condemned. He then often lies to us that it is God who is doing the condemning **Revelation 12:10**.

Unfortunately, we also are experts at condemning ourselves without the enemy's help. Our own insecurities or shame can provoke thoughts or emotions telling us *woe is me* or *I am less-than, not worthy, or not enough.* On the other hand, our pride or shame can bring self-condemnation, telling us: *I should be perfect!*

> *Seeing then that we have a great High Priest who has passed through the heavens, Jesus the Son of God, let us hold fast our confession.*
>
> *For we do not have a High Priest who cannot sympathize with our weaknesses, but was in all points tempted as we are, yet without sin.*
>
> *Let us therefore come boldly to the throne of grace that we may obtain mercy and find grace to help in time of need.*
> **Hebrews 4:14-16**

Condemnation causes us to turn our faces away from God in shame, guilt, and frustration. Instead, the convicting work of the Spirit encourages us wholeheartedly to the arms of our Heavenly Daddy to ask His forgiveness and seek His help.

> *That there is no condemnation for those who are in Christ Jesus, who do not walk according to the flesh but according to the Spirit.*
> **Romans 8:1**
>
> *For if our heart condemns us, God is greater than our heart, and knows all things.*
> **1 John 3:20**

Conviction of Righteousness:

Next, we read that the Holy Spirit convinces the world of *righteousness* because Jesus relates that He is returning to the Father. Simply put, the resurrection of Jesus Christ proves His absolute sinlessness, righteousness, and ability to grant righteousness by faith to those who believe Him. Jesus was able to annihilate death because death and hell could find nothing to hold onto in the righteous, sinless Savior **Hebrews 2:14.**

Dikaios Greek—Meaning: *Just, righteous, upright, the fulfillment of God's rightness.*

Jesus is the only One who can claim the righteousness of God, and He has the backing of the Father and the Spirit Who raised Him from the dead. The resurrection proves that Jesus was and is God **Philippians 2:7-11.** This convincing work of the Spirit tells sinners that they have missed the mark and need the One and Only, Jesus Christ, and His resurrection proves the integrity and truth of His words. This passage also takes us a step further because the Spirit not only convinces us of Christ's righteousness but the reality that His righteousness has been imputed to us as well, to redeem us and set us free from our sin **Romans 4:22-25.**

> *For He made Him who knew no sin to be sin for us, that we might become the righteousness of God in Him.*
> **2 Corinthians 5:21**

Oh! The depth of love God has for us that He would place our sin on His Son to reconcile us to Himself. Then He clothes us in His righteousness when our own righteousness is, at best, like putrid and filthy rags.

Conviction of Judgment:

The Holy Spirit convinces the world of judgment because the ruler of this world has already been judged **John 12:31, John 16:11, Daniel 7:22.** The enemy's defeat in the wilderness to bring down the Son of God was thwarted. Because Jesus did not give in to temptation, He can rightfully (righteously) claim the title of the spotless, unblemished Lamb of God—the final and ultimate sacrifice for the redemption of humanity. Not only did Jesus secure redemption for all who would believe, but He secured the condemnation and *eternal judgment* of Satan **Colossians 2:13-15**.

We are armed with Jesus' authority.

Yes, Satan's judgment is secure, and he is defeated. Nevertheless, his sentence of punishment won't be carried out until the end of this age of human history **Revelation 20:10**. In the meantime—*the time in which we live*—the world is still under the sway of the adversary **1 John 5:19**.

Now, it is the believer's great privilege to press the judgment of the adversary's defeat upon him as we are armed with the authority of Jesus' name and as we move forward as vessels of the Holy Spirit, bringing heaven down to earth wherever we go **Acts 3:16**. Pastor Jack Hayford writes:

> *...the foundational fact remains that an agelong struggle between "the saints" and the power of evil in the world calls each believer to a commitment to steadfast battle, a mixture of victories with setbacks, and a consummate triumph anticipated at Christ's coming. In the meantime, we "receive" the kingdom and pursue victories for our King, by His power, making intermittent gains—all of which are based on "the judgment" achieved through the Cross **Daniel 7:18, 21-22**.[2]*

Accomplishing this ongoing work of Jesus through us makes it imperative that we learn to walk in Holy Spirit fulness in all His supernatural gifts and be transformed by Him to walk in all His fruitfulness **1 Corinthians 12:8-10, Galatians 5:22-25**.

He has delivered us from the power of darkness and conveyed
us into the kingdom of the Son of His love.
Colossians 1:13 (Parentheses, mine)

Continuing Through John:

As we proceed through **John 16:12-15**, Jesus interjects His discourse by telling the disciples that He still has many things to say to them, but they are not in a place to bear or be able to handle more that He has to say. Remember, they still hadn't experienced the Holy Spirit indwelling them. If you have experienced something phenomenal, but you try to relate the experience to someone who hasn't walked that road yet, you are somewhat limited in what you can share. We can imagine that many things that Jesus told the disciples during His earthly ministry made more sense after the resurrection when they could see the redemption story in its entirety in conjunction with the Old Testament and the power of the Holy Spirit.

Jesus teaches His followers that the Holy Spirit is the *Spirit of truth* and that He will guide them into *all* truth. This revealing of all truth perfectly coincides with Jesus stating that the Holy Spirit would take all of who He is, what He has, what He has accomplished, and what He does, and reveal these things to His followers because *Jesus Himself is Truth*. Jesus doesn't just speak the truth—*He is the Truth speaking* **John 14:6**.[3] This revealing work of the Holy Spirit is so essential to the Christian that Jesus states it twice **John 16:14, 15**.

In John's first letter, he wrote to believers enticed by false teaching:

These things I have written to you concerning those who try
to deceive you.

But the anointing which you have received from Him abides
in you and you do not need that anyone teach you; but as the
same anointing teaches you concerning all things, and is true,

and is not a lie, and just as it has taught you, you will abide in Him.
1 John 2:26-27

The anointing in this passage is the anointing of the Spirit upon a believer's life. Notice the use of the word *all* again in these verses. The Holy Spirit is the Spirit of truth and stands in complete opposition to the *spirit of error* in the world **1 John 4:4-6**.

We each have Holy Spirit anointing.

From the same portion of scripture above, we learn that we can rely upon the Holy Spirit to teach us. However, God has placed the much-needed offices of *teachers* and *pastors* in the church **Ephesians 4:11-12**. Nevertheless, the Holy Spirit of truth can inform us if a human teacher is in error. By the measure of God's Word and His Spirit inside us, we can have confidence in walking in God's truth in any situation as we ask Him for guidance and choose to follow His direction.

Again, we find in John's writings the unity of the Godhead. God is relational to the core of His being. Although the Spirit will not speak on His own authority, He is still entirely God. Let it warm our hearts without end to be called into fellowship with God, just as the Three have fellowship with one another **John 15:9-10, 26.**

The promises to believers found in **John 16:13-15** are:

- The Holy Spirit will come.
- He will guide us into all truth.
- He will tell us things to come.
- He will glorify Jesus—in our lives and aid our worship.
- He will take what is of Jesus and declare it to us.

In **John 15**, we discover that we can do absolutely nothing of eternal value outside a sweet and abiding relationship with the Lord that far surpasses casualness. That doesn't mean we work harder but find all strength and resources as we rest in Him.

God is after more for us. He sends His Spirit so the work that Jesus began to do of bringing His kingdom to earth will continue. The Holy Spirit causes Jesus' presence to be experienced in our lives so that we might have the most tender and loving relationship with Him with the natural overflow of bringing Him glory. And the more we offer ourselves to the Holy Spirit's work in our lives will reveal Jesus to those in our weary world so that they might know true purpose, ultimate satisfaction, deep healing, and glorious salvation.

However, I am telling you nothing but the truth
when I say it is profitable (good, expedient, advantageous)
for you that I go away.
Because if I do not go away,
the Comforter
(Counselor, Helper, Advocate, Intercessor, Strengthener,
Standby)
will not come to you [into close fellowship with you];
but if I go away, I will send Him to you
[to be in close fellowship with you].
John 16:7 AMPC

---

[1] Joyce Meyer, Your Battles Belong to the Lord (New York, NY; FaithWrods Hachette Book Group, 2019), pages 110-111.

[2] Jack Hayford, Litt.D., Executive Editor, *Spirit-Filled Life Bible, Third Edition* (Nashville, TN; Thomas Nelson, 2018), page 1175, Kingdom Dynamics, Daniel 7:21-22, by Jack Hayford.

[3] Quote from the late Pastor Jerry Cook. Time reference unknown.

Study Questions:

- What spoke to you most from this chapter?

- Elaborate below what means for you to have the *advantage* of the Holy Spirit in your life.

- From the definition of *Parakletos*—a name of the Holy Spirit—found on *page 36,* what word or phrase encourages you and why?

- Is knowing the difference between Holy Spirit conviction and the enemy's condemnation helpful? Explain.

- Look back at the bullet points on *page 43* regarding the Holy Spirit's promises to believers. Which one of these speaks to your heart most and why?

4

The Holy Spirit
in You

We have been introduced to the Holy Spirit in both the Old and New Testaments. Now, we will examine some of the ways He works *in* our lives as believers, setting the stage for our coming chapters. It will be essential for us to note that the Holy Spirit is key to our identity in Jesus and confirms that we are truly His. Please keep this in mind as we ponder these verses.

In **John 7:37-39**, on the last day of the Hebrew celebration, the *Feast of Tabernacles*, Lord Jesus cries out some of the most thrilling words regarding the Holy Spirit in the Scriptures. Read this passage carefully, noting all you learn and what is speaking to your heart.

_____

_____

_____

_____

_____

Read **John 20:19-22**, focusing on **verses 21** and **22**. What happened?

_____

The Lord does something that at first glance may seem unusual, but having learned that one of the definitions of the word Spirit in the original Greek means *breath or to breathe*, does Jesus' action make more sense? Why is that?

_____

_____

2 Corinthians 1:21-22 and **Ephesians 1:12-14** are Paul's words to the early church, and these two passages are very similar. What does Paul communicate regarding the Holy Spirit that is meaningful to your life as a Christ-follower?

_____

_____

_____

Depending on what version of the Bible you are using, there is a common word or phrase in the previous two texts. What is it?

_____

Share what it means to know the Holy Spirit is a *pledge* or *guarantee* of your inheritance in Christ.

_____

_____

_____

Read **Romans 5:5** about the Holy Spirit revealing God's love for you. Capture below what knowing this truth speaks to your heart.

_____

_____

Paul has powerful words for us in **Romans 8:9-13**. What does he say is the difference between *believers* and *unbelievers* in Jesus?

_____

_____

_____

Paul moves from very direct verbiage to very tender wording in **Romans 8:14-17**, telling us both about the Holy Spirit's work in our lives along with a few powerful promises. Please record what you learn from this passage. Again, don't be concerned about filling in every line.

- _____

- _____

- _____

- _____

- _____

- _____

- _____

- _____

Take another look at **Romans 8:16**. Describe what it means for you to have the Holy Spirit confirm that you are God's child.

_____

_____

_____

The New Testament gives several references that every person who receives the Lord Jesus by faith immediately experiences the indwelling of the Holy Spirit. We have looked at a few of these passages, making the case that *the Holy Spirit fills all believers*. Read **1 Corinthians 2:10-16**.

These verses are similar to what we read in our previous chapter from **John 16:8-15.** Please jot down any similarities you find.

- _____
- _____
- _____
- _____
- _____

Let's look at one of Jesus' last statements to the disciples before ascending into heaven that will prepare us for the next chapter. Read **Luke 24:49.** Rewrite the verse in your own words.

_____

_____

_____

_____

Now, compare the verse above with what you read earlier in **John 20:21-22.** Ponder the two passages and draw some conclusions of your own.

_____

_____

_____

_____

Could this possibly mean that there is a _second experience_ for the believer concerning the Holy Spirit? What do you think and why?

_____

_____

_____

Rivers of Living Water...

When Jesus emphatically spoke of the Holy Spirit as the source of living water to the thirsty soul in **John 7:37-39**, He gave us a glimpse of living our lives daily in the Spirit. He significantly spoke His words on the last day of the Feast of Tabernacles, where the priests daily poured out water on the temple altar throughout the celebration as a symbolic remembrance of the water supplied from the rock in **Exodus 17:6**.

As we carefully consider Jesus' words, we realize that the swift current of a flowing river—its strength and cleansing, and sustaining properties—applies perfectly to the work of the Holy Spirit to satisfy our lives and reveal Christ through us. And who has ever stepped into the midst of a river and not experienced its movement?

Let's live in the Holy Spirit's river.

Paul takes this a step further when he describes Jesus as the *Rock* from whom the river flows:

> *...and all drank the same spiritual drink. For they drank of that spiritual Rock that followed them, and that Rock was Christ.*
> **1 Corinthians 10:4**

It is thrilling to imagine all that must have happened on the glorious day when Jesus rose from the dead. We read in **John 20:19-22** that Jesus appears behind closed doors to His disciples who gathered because of the fear of reprisal for being Jesus' followers. We also find this meeting recorded in **Luke 24:36**. However, it is only noted in John's gospel that Jesus breathes on them and tells them to *receive the Holy Spirit* **John 20:22**. Knowing that the Greek word *pneuma* used here for the Holy Spirit has the meaning of *breath* or to *breathe*, and remembering what we've read in **Genesis 2:7** about the *breath of life*, this little quoted verse is rich with meaning.

As we think this through, we realize this wondrous incident is the first opportunity that Jesus' followers have to experience salvation. The Old Testament prophecies regarding the death and resurrection of the Messiah for humanity's salvation were just fulfilled. Jesus then breathes on those gathered and initiates the working and indwelling of the Spirit *in* their lives that has been present throughout His earthly ministry.

Missionary Reinhard Bonnke writes:

> *There were many caesars and rulers...the religious and political elite of their day. But Jesus bypassed them all and went to lowly fishermen and tax collectors – the uneducated, uncultured traders by the sea of Galilee. Some had cheated and one had stolen, but because they were pliable and yielding, He could shape them into world changers, and He did. To this day, Jesus is still doing the same using men and women from all backgrounds. He cleanses them with His blood, empowers them by His Spirit and uses them as world changers. You can be one of them too: living fire.[1]*

Holy Spirit Guarantee...

When we look at **2 Corinthians 1:21-22** and **Ephesians 1:12-14** together, Paul writes that the Holy Spirit of promise seals believers as the *guarantee* of their inheritance. Oh, how encouraging these verses are as we sense the Holy Spirit boundlessly encouraging us that God seals us for eternity as His children.

Let's take a look at the Greek word for *guarantee*:

Arrabon Greek—Meaning: A *guarantee, pledge, deposit, down payment, or security.*

Consider it this way. Jesus has made full payment for our redemption with His sacrificial death. The Holy Spirit then acts as a seal or a *down payment* on our lives as we receive our inheritance in Jesus here on earth and our entire inheritance in heaven **Ephesians 1:18**.

The Greek word *arrabon* also describes an engagement or wedding ring. What another beautiful type of the Holy Spirit's seal upon our lives as we ponder Him as Jesus' pledge to us that we will partake of the great marriage supper of the Lamb as the bride of Christ **Revelation 19:7-9**.

Dr. Steve Schell writes…

> *In ancient cultures, seals were a common part of life. The person who carried a seal carried with them the authority of the one who sent them…*
>
> *By calling the Holy Spirit a "pledge (arrabon) of our inheritance," Paul is saying that God has given the Holy Spirit to us with such evident power that this gift is like a down payment. Our experience with the Spirit now is so real, so tangible, and so observable that it proves God will give us the full measure of our inheritance when Jesus returns to set up God's kingdom on earth.*[2]

We read in **Romans 5:5** that the love of God has been *shed abroad in our hearts*. Notice that the word used here is about our *hearts*, not our *minds*. We can know about God's love for us intellectually, which is vital for our decision to receive His limitless love and follow Him. Nevertheless, when we *experience* His love within our hearts, an exhilarating dimension is added to our walk with Him. With the gentle, warm breeze of His Spirit within our now alive spirit, we sense His felt *nearness, strength, comfort, and love* in our emotions.

The experience of His felt presence coupled with the anchoring foundation of God's Word in our lives will see us through any tempest or storm of the enemy, the world, or any difficult circumstances that Paul writes about in **Romans 5:3-5**.

Maureen Broderson writes this concerning the power of the Holy Spirit in spiritual warfare and for our everyday lives:

> *One of the greatest blessings of all is Christ did not leave us alone to fight this (spiritual) war. He left us Himself in the person of the Holy Spirit—not a percentage of the Holy Spirit, not a junior Holy Spirit. At the very moment we received Christ as our Savior and Lord, the same Holy Spirit who raised Jesus Christ from the dead became alive in us.*
>
> *The immediacy of His presence equips and empowers us to live our lives, with all of our unique personal challenges, as Jesus would live them. Astonishing, isn't it?[3]*

Paul doesn't shortchange words when he speaks of the Holy Spirit residing in the life of every believer in contrast with those who don't yet know the Lord by faith **Romans 8:9, 1 Corinthians 3:16**. Yet, we as believers must remember that the Holy Spirit *bears witness* or *affirms* with our spirit that we are God's children.

We have Holy Spirit fullness.

> *For his Spirit joins with our spirit to affirm that we are God's children.*
> **Romans 8:16** NLT

No, we don't base our salvation upon what we are feeling at any given moment. Instead, we stand upon the immovable rock of God's Word. Yet, we can be confident in *realizing* the Holy Spirit is drawing us close as children to our Father by the confirming sense of His presence. This resonance of the Holy Spirit within our spirit will also be vital as we learn in future chapters about the supernatural gifts of the Holy Spirit. Then, the Spirit will confirm or bear witness deep within us that He is prompting us to step out in trust with what He is either speaking or showing us.

Discerning the Holy Spirit's affirmation regarding spiritual gifts may take some practice, but it is well worth our continual, heartfelt pursuit of His leading.

What promises we find in **Romans 8:14-17** for the Christian!

- The Spirit will lead us—if we let Him!
- We did not receive a spirit of fear or bondage.
- We have received the Spirit of adoption.
- The Spirit affirms in our spirits that we are God's children
- We are heirs of God.
- We are joint heirs with Christ.
- Though we will experience suffering, we will be glorified with Him.

Holy Spirit Breath...

Pivotal to our study now is the timing between what Jesus' disciples experienced on the day of His resurrection and what took place fifty days later at the Feast of Pentecost. We read in **John 20:22** that Jesus breathed upon His followers, inviting them to *receive* the Holy Spirit.

The Promise of the Father.

Lambano Greek—Meaning: *To receive, gain, get, obtain, to get back. To lay hold of, to take upon one's self, to claim, procure.*

Then, after this experience with the Lord on resurrection day, Luke writes that just before Jesus' ascension into heaven, He told the disciples:

Behold, I send the Promise of My Father upon you; but tarry

*in the city of Jerusalem until you are endued with **power from
on high.***
Luke 24:49 (repeated in **Acts 1:4, 8,** emphasis mine)

Jesus' words clearly speak of a second experience with the Holy Spirit in
addition to His followers already receiving the Spirit when He breathed on
them earlier. The indicator of this second experience is the endowment of
power: *dynamis.*

The disciples have received the breath of Jesus' life, the seal of the Holy
Spirit; now they are to wait for the overflow of the Spirit's power before
commencing with the great commission: to go into all the world, preaching
the gospel **Matthew 28:18-20, Luke 24:47**. Jesus tells them that the good
news of God's love will be demonstrated by the Promise of the Father for
working signs and wonders through the disciples' hands **Mark 16:15-20**.
The disciples have received the gentle breath of the Holy Spirit in bringing
life to their spirits. It is now time for the Holy Spirit to baptize them with
His power!

---

[1] Reinhard Bonnke, *Holy Spirit: Are We Flammable or Fireproof?* (Orlando, FL; Christ
for All Nations, 2017) page 124.

[2] Dr. Steve Schell, *The Promise of the Father: Understanding and Receiving the Baptism
With the Holy Spirit* (Federal Way, WA; Life Lessons Publishing) pages 86-87.

[3] Maureen Broderson, *Victorious Spiritual Warfare, So Simple, Grandma Can Do It*
(Washington D.C.; Vide Press, 2021) pages 6-7.

Study Questions:

- What spoke to you most from this chapter?

- Explain what *rivers of living water* in the Holy Spirit means to your life.

- The Holy Spirit is the believer's guarantee, confirming they are God's child. How does this touch your heart?

- Which one of the promises that are bulleted on pages 53 speak to your life currently and why?

- What are your thoughts regarding the second experience of the Holy Spirit for a Jesus follower?

5

The Promise
of the
Father

The men and women in the Book of Acts have nothing on us.

No. They really don't. They weren't superhuman, but they experienced the supernatural moving of the Holy Spirit. They, like us now, were products of a fallen race—broken, confused, wounded, and prideful. However, these early Christians lived Spirit-filled lives that turned the world upside-down, or more correctly, right-side up!

Yes, many of them were eyewitnesses of Jesus' majesty, walking the dusty roads with Him **2 Peter 1:16**. They were on hand to see all of His miraculous works, His compassion, kindness, and infinite love. But many in the early church didn't see Him in person. They were as we are—*who have not seen and yet believed* **John 20:29b**. These Book of Acts participants, a mixture of eyewitnesses and those who didn't personally see Jesus, were flesh and blood men and women with dreams, fears, families, businesses, failures, and successes. They had the same hang-ups and stresses as we do, if not more so. They, too, had to pay the mortgage, put food on the table, and keep up with the kids. They were just like us now—desperate, knowing that they couldn't do this thing called *life* alone without some powerful help.

Somehow, even as a young believer in my staid traditional church background, I sensed that Christ-followers could experience the New Testament power of the Holy Spirit. In my early teens, I encountered Him, changing the course of my life. Since that marvelous day, I have been ruined for anything less than seeing the Spirit moving in my life and the lives of others. Now, many years later, I am even more compelled to know God more profoundly, and with the Spirit's anointing and leading, to herald the truth that His power is not diminished to heal physically, emotionally, and mentally. To share with others that what we would term *extraordinary* could actually be *ordinary* for a believer. And what we would define as *supernatural* can be our *natural* way of life: not hyped, hyper, weird, or scary.

Let's now examine the *Promise of the Father* that Jesus speaks of right before His ascension into heaven. Then, we will journey through various events recorded in the Book of Acts. We will also draw from what we have learned about the Holy Spirit residing in the life of a believer from our previous chapter. The ultimate question we will ask consists of three words: *is there more?*

Turn to one of these passages that share John the Baptist's prophetic words: **Matthew 3:11, Mark 1:8, Luke 3:16, John 1:33**. Convey below what you think he is trying to communicate when he speaks about Holy Spirit baptism, considering aspects of water baptism.

_____

_____

_____

Open to **Luke 24:46-49**. Here, Lord Jesus presents to His followers the Great Commission for sharing His gospel worldwide. Looking specifically at **verse 49**, share why you think the Lord told the disciples to wait or tarry for the *Promise of the Father* before moving forward with His directives.

_____

_____

_____

Recognizing that Luke the Physician pens the Book of Acts as a continuation of the Gospel of Luke, look at **Acts 1:4-8** and record what strikes you as significant statements.

- _____

- _____

- _____

- _____

- _____

- _____

- _____

List key words from your statements above:

_____

_____

Turn to **Acts 2:1-13** to read about the _Promise of the Father_ descending on the disciples during the Jewish celebration, Pentecost. What especially amazes you or grabs your attention as you read?

_____

_____

_____

Immediately upon receiving the baptism in the Holy Spirit, the once fearful Peter, who previously had denied knowing Christ, now preaches the sermon of his life **Acts 2:15-39**. Though it is a lengthy passage, it is worthy of careful reading. Peter concludes his message in **verses 38-39**. What do his closing words here speak to your heart concerning the Holy Spirit and your life?

_____

_____

The Spirit's moving upon listening ears is evident in **verse 37**, with the outcome shared in **verse 41**. What takes place immediately following Peter's message?

_____

_____

Acts 3:1-11 relates a beautiful story of the extension of God's healing love for a paralyzed beggar through Peter and John. These two men are subsequently arrested for preaching and healing in Jesus' name. Read **Acts 4:8-14**. What is the conclusion reached by the temple rulers regarding Peter and John? How are their words significant for our lives?

_____

_____

Next, the temple guard released Peter and John from custody. The disciples return to the greater gathering of believers and pray specifically to continue to preach the gospel with signs and wonders confirming the gospel's truth in Jesus' name **Acts 4:23-31**. Can you draw a parallel to **Acts 4:31** and **Luke 24:49** about the waiting for the enduement of the Holy Spirit's power?

_____

_____

Acts 8:14-23 marks the beginning of four events recorded in the Book of Acts that will cause us to think hard about a second experience with the Spirit in addition to His initial infilling of our spirits at our point of salvation. Please read these passages and share what strikes you as important about each event with the new believers. Prayerfully consider God's working in these passages:

Acts 8:14-23

_____

_____

Acts 9:17

_____

_____

Acts 10:44-48

_____

_____

Acts 11:12-18 _Peter's account of the previous verses_

_____

_____

Acts 19:1-7

_____

_____

Open up **Luke 11:9-13**. Our concluding passage in this study chapter is a promise Jesus gives regarding the Holy Spirit. This promise has the same certainty as the promise of salvation for those who receive Christ by faith found in **John 1:12**. What is the promise spoken of here?

_____

_____

_____

Book of Acts Living...

Book of Acts living. Why would we settle for less? Well, for lots of reasons. Fear is probably the chief reason of all. The problem is we have a dying world at stake.

The world hungers to experience God.

A world hungry for experiencing God, not mere theory about Him. A world yearning for His loving power, not pious platitudes. This same world that needs heaven's touch because it has been hell-bent since Adam and Eve handed it over to the king of hell.

Many years ago, I was in such tremendous need of the Holy Spirit in my own life, let alone considering His help in the lives of others. Something in my heart cried out to God for more when I was just a youth. Now, more than ever, I invite the Holy Spirit to pour through me daily as I learn to hear His voice more distinctly, take action when I sense His promptings, and take daily steps forward in my own personal growth and freedom. Do I stumble and fall at times? Yes, of course! Nevertheless, I can hardly recognize the insecure, broken, and bound young woman I once was.

Back to Book of Acts living. Let's look again at Peter's final words to the crowd gathered on the Day of Pentecost when the Holy Spirit came as the Promise of the Father:

> *...and you shall receive the gift of the Holy Spirit. For the promise is to you and to your children, and to all who are afar off, as many as the Lord our God will call.*
> **Acts 2:38-39**

To as many as the Lord our God will call. Peter is preaching about all who would respond to the good news of Jesus Christ and give their lives to follow Him through the ages. There is no limit or end date spoken of here.

Our opening verses all state the same message foretelling that Jesus would baptize His followers in the Spirit and with fire **Matthew 3:11, Mark 1:8, Luke 3:16, John 1:33.**

Holy Spirit Baptism...

What does the word *baptism* mean in the original Greek?

Baptizo Greek–Meaning: *To baptize, dip, dye, immerse, plunge, submerge, inundate, flood, swamp, soak, douse, drench, or saturate.*

How does this definition touch your heart? Is there a particular word or two that speaks to your louder than the others? These are not passive words: *immerse, plunge, submerge, inundate, dye, and flood.* They are strong statements regarding what Jesus would accomplish in our lives by sending the Holy Spirit to live within us.

God's Word often speaks in word pictures and analogies. He wants to soak and drench us, yet, at that same time, set us ablaze!

God desires to drench us and set us ablaze!

The previous chapter of our study establishes that the disciples received the Holy Spirit when Jesus *breathed* upon them on the day of His resurrection **John 20:22**. We also know that since that day, every believer in Christ has received the Holy Spirit's life breath in their spirit and been *born again* spiritually.

Please recall **Luke 24:49** and its repetition in **Acts 1:4**. Although Jesus' disciples were filled with the Spirit, He told them to wait for the *Promise of the Father* before beginning their ministry. Jesus further elaborates in **Acts 1:8** about the equipping of the *dynamis-power* for their testimony and witness of His gospel.

It is interesting to note that Jesus speaks of the Spirit as *coming upon* them rather than *in* them. In **Ephesians 5:18**, Paul encourages us to continue being *filled* with the Spirit, although his other writings tell us we are *always* filled with the Spirit as believers. These various words are not contradictory in their usage. Believers can experience the presence of the Holy Spirit *in, upon,* or *being filled*.

This illustration might be helpful:

Take a large pitcher of water and pour it into a drinking glass to the brim representing the initial infilling of the Spirit into a believer's now born-again spirit. Next, aim directly into the glass and pour the remaining water from the pitcher. The water from the pitcher is now *coming upon* and replenishing the water *already in* the glass, causing that water to overflow, be continually filled, and renewed. By now, water should be gushing over the sides of the glass and splattering everywhere!

Jesus tells the disciples to wait for *dynamis-power* to come upon them and overflow them before they start the great commission of spreading the good news of the kingdom. When we are living our lives and ministering out of the Holy Spirit's overflow within us, He has a significant effect on everyone we are around.

Last week, I demonstrated this illustration with the pitcher of water and the filled glass to a group of students and staff at a Youth with a Mission base (YWAM) in Taiwan. As the water from the pitcher rained down upon the filled glass, it sprayed outward several feet. The first row of students felt the water's impact! This illustration reminded them how far-reaching the ministry of the Holy Spirit can be if we let Him baptize, inundate, saturate, overflow, and empower our lives.

Here are a few of the statements that Jesus makes about the Holy Spirit to His disciples in **Acts 1:4-8**:

- They must wait in Jerusalem for the Promise of the Father.

- John baptized only in water, but they also needed Spirit baptism.
- This event will take place shortly.
- They would receive *dynamis* when the Spirit comes upon them.
- Because of that *dynamis-power*, they will be witnesses of His Gospel to the ends of the earth.

God's timing is perfect. However, our hearts might challenge this statement at times! Nevertheless, we can look back over our lives and see how much we would have missed that He had in store for us if He had worked on our timetable. The same is true for His timing for the first release of the Holy Spirit upon the disciples—the *Promise of the Father*. Possibly, the seemingly long wait of several weeks to receive the Spirit's overflow was arduous for the disciples. Nevertheless, God's timing was impeccable.

Pentecost...

What we know as the *Day of Pentecost*—derived from the Hebrew word for fifty, *pentekoste*—was the Hebrew celebration of *the Feast of Weeks* or the *Feast of First Fruits*. God chose this feast to pour out His Spirit. This particular celebration *was exactly* seven weeks, plus one day (fifty days) after the celebration of the Jewish *Passover* when Christ, our sacrificial Lamb, was crucified **Leviticus 23:15-22**. One of three feasts in the Jewish calendar that Hebrews were required to attend, God knew that multitudes from various nations would gather in Jerusalem and be present to hear the gospel of Jesus Christ preached for the first time after His resurrection.

God chose this Hebrew holiday that celebrated the first buds or first fruits of Israel's agricultural harvest to demonstrate the power of the Holy Spirit to bring about spiritual *first fruits*—the first believers and the first harvest of souls—in Jesus.

*Of His own will He brought us forth by the word of truth, that
we might be a kind of firstfruits of His creatures.*
James 1:18 (emphasis added)

As the disciples—both men and women—were gathered, most likely in a
tented rooftop structure or an upper room with open windows, the sound
of a rushing, mighty wind filled their meeting room, the very description
of Holy Spirit wind or breath. This was not the noise of a balmy breeze.
The disciples also saw flames or tongues of fire sitting upon each of their
heads as the Holy Spirit poured out upon them.

These flames of fire are significant. From the Greek rendering in this
passage, it is unclear if these were actual flames, or something seen in the
prophetic sense of seeing a vision. This uncertainty doesn't undermine the
miracle of what happened because it appears that most or all those in that
upper room saw the same thing and would have recognized its importance.

Dr. Steve Schell elaborates further about the Spirit's phenomena on the
day of Pentecost:

> *...a pillar of fire appeared over each disciple's head, and that
> pillar of fire was a symbol every Jewish believer would have
> recognized immediately. They had been taught since they
> were children that when Moses prepared the tabernacle in the
> wilderness, the Lord demonstrated that He had come to dwell
> in that tabernacle by placing over it a cloud by day and a
> pillar of fire by night.[1] So, on Pentecost when fire appeared
> over every head, those disciples understood what God was
> saying to them: "This is now My tabernacle...Here is my
> dwelling place..."[2]*

Immediately, they began to speak the glorious praises of God in other
tongues or languages not previously known to them as a learned
language **Acts 2:11**. The ruckus and joy of the upper room had likely
spilled to the streets below as those attending the feast from distant lands

heard God's praises in their native languages causing them to inquire if the Christians were actually drunk! We will take an in-depth look at this spiritual gifting of the Holy Spirit in the next chapter of our study.

As we continue reading **Acts 2**, we view the once cowardly Peter preaching the lordship of Jesus to several thousand people gathered in Jerusalem for the feast with a passion, fire, and power he had not known before. Although the Lord had told Peter and the other disciples to wait in Jerusalem before the day of Pentecost,

The Promise of the Father transforms us.

Peter had returned to Galilee to his old fishing vocation **John 21:3**. After an encounter with Christ on the shores of Galilee, Peter headed back to Jerusalem to wait in obedience for the *Promise of the Father*. It appears that Peter had left the upper room and seized the opportunity to preach to the multitudes who were probably gathering on the Jerusalem temple's southern steps. This temple area formed an amphitheater for the listeners wanting an explanation of what was happening.

Peter, and all those with him, experienced a radical encounter and transformation on this day of the Feast of First Fruits or Pentecost.

Matthew Henry's Commentary, published in 1706, states:

> *We have seen the wonderful effect of the pouring out of the Spirit, in its influence upon the preachers of the gospel. Peter, in all his life, never spoke at the rate that he had done now, with such fullness, perspicuity, and power.*

> *We are now to see another blessed fruit of the pouring out of the Spirit in its influence upon the hearers of the gospel. From the first delivery of that divine message, it appeared that there was a divine power going along with it, and it was mighty, through God, to do wonders: thousands were immediately*

*brought by it to the obedience of faith; it was the rod of God's strength sent out of Zion, **Psalm 110:2-3.***

*We have here the first-fruits of that vast harvest of souls which by it were gathered in to Jesus Christ. Come and see, in these verses, the exalted Redeemer riding forth, in these chariots of salvation, conquering and to conquer, **Revelation 6:2.**[3]*

Holy Spirit baptism is for everyone.

Peter preached the sermon of his life that day in Jerusalem in the *dynamis* of the Spirit. He concluded his impromptu message by calling his listeners to repentance and faith in Christ. Three thousand men—not including women and children—responded during this amazing altar call. Peter then promises the new converts that they, too, will receive the gift of the Holy Spirit just as they have seen and heard the disciples in the streets moments earlier. This *Promise of the Father* is not only for Jesus' initial disciples. It is for everyone who calls upon the Lord in repentance, to their children, and to all who are *afar off* or would come to faith after them, including us today.

For the promise is to you and to your children, and to all who are afar off, as many as the Lord our God will call.
Acts 2:39

The day of Pentecost initiates the ministry of preaching the Kingdom of God with confirming signs and wonders, as the Book of Acts records. From that momentous day forward, we read in Luke's account numerous stories of miracles taking place of every size and shape in the early church. There is no going back to the mundane for those who walk with Jesus!

More Encounters in Acts...

The outpouring or baptism of the Holy Spirit did not end with the disciples on that eventful day of the Feast of First Fruits. We close this chapter of our study with four more recorded accounts of the Holy Spirit's overflow in believers' lives as a second experience.

In **Acts 8:14-22**, when the apostles in Jerusalem heard that Samaria had received the word of God, they sent Peter and John to that region to pray for the new believers that they might receive the Spirit's overflow. So powerful was the encounter that a local sorcerer inquired about purchasing this ability. Peter soundly rebukes the man.

Rev. Dennis and Rita Bennett write:

> *When the apostles at Jerusalem heard of this new breakthrough in Samaria (folk were coming to faith in Jesus), they sent Peter and John to see what was taking place. As soon as these two arrived, they saw something lacking. The Holy Spirit wasn't "falling upon" or overwhelming these new believers...*

> *The Holy Spirit was already indwelling these Samaritan believers. He was ready to inundate their souls and bodies, to baptize, to overflow, but they had to respond, to receive. As soon as they did, the Holy Spirit began to pour out from them just as He had with the first believers on the Day of Pentecost.[4]*

We read about Paul's dramatic conversion on the road to Damascus. He had a firsthand encounter with the Savior as he was on his way to imprison and kill Jesus' followers. The Lord then instructs another believer to find Paul, release him from the blindness of His Christ-encounter by the laying on of hands, and to receive the baptism of the Holy Spirit. Paul, at this point, had already proclaimed Jesus as Lord **Acts 9:1-18**.

Next, we find Peter preaching to the Gentile household of Cornelius. The latter immediately received the word of salvation and were promptly filled with the baptism of the Holy Spirit with the evidence of speaking in tongues **Acts 10:44-48**.

Finally, we read of Paul passing through the upper territory of Ephesus and finding new Christians who had only experienced John the Baptist's baptism of repentance. However, they hadn't yet heard about or had an understanding regarding the Holy Spirit. Paul immediately baptized them in water in the name of Jesus and laid hands on them, whereby they spoke in tongues and prophesied **Acts 19:1-7**.

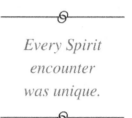

Every Spirit encounter was unique.

Every encounter was unique. The only prerequisites were belief in the Savior, having an expectant heart, and simply asking.

> *If you then, being evil, know how to give good gifts to your children, how much more will your heavenly Father give the Holy Spirit to those who ask Him!*
> **Luke 11:13**

I think one thing we can all agree upon when reading the accounts of Christians encountering the Holy Spirit—He made a difference in their lives. Something of substance took place—something the flesh could not manufacture. The Spirit's overflow in these folks, just like us, would be just as Jesus said—*rivers of living water*—not only to refresh and empower their own lives but to purposely work through them in demonstrations of His love and power to bring others to salvation.

Before we continue learning how simple it is to invite the Holy Spirit to baptize us, we will look at one of the most misunderstood aspects of this teaching: the spiritual gift of *speaking in tongues*. Take some time to answer the questions provided here. Then we will move forward.

---

[1] Exodus 40:34-38

[2] Dr. Steve Schell, *The Promise of the Father: Understanding and Receiving the Baptism with the Holy Spirit* (Federal Way, Washington; Life Lessons Publishing, 2020), page 32.

[3] Matthew Henry, *Matthew Henry's Commentary on the Whole Bible-Volume VI Acts to Revelation* (Old Tappan, MJ; Fleming H. Revell Company, 1935), note at Acts 2:37, page25.

[4] Dennis and Rita Bennett, The Holy Spirit and You; A Study-Guide to the Spirit-Filled Life (Plainfield, NJ; Logos International, 1971), page 30.

Study Questions:

- What spoke to you most from this chapter?

- Look at the words that define the Greek word *baptizo* on *page 63*. Which one of those words speaks to you? Ponder that word further and share what comes to your heart.

- What are your thoughts about God's timing for the *Promise of the Father* to descend on Pentecost or the Feast of First Fruits?

- Think about Peter's life from the Gospels. Then consider his powerfully anointed sermon on the temple steps. What are your thoughts about this?

- Looking at the other four encounters mentioned in Acts about the Holy Spirit's baptism, how are you encouraged for your own life?

6

To Speak or
Not to Speak...

The Holy Spirit's *gift of speaking in tongues* or a *heavenly* or *spiritual language* (we will use these terms interchangeably in our study) has often aroused various feelings in Christians throughout the years. From one end of the spectrum that discounts the experience entirely or attributes it to the enemy of our souls, to the middle of the same spectrum that views this as a powerful and beautiful gift that the Holy Spirit provides to a believer. And, of course, we can swing to the opposite end of the range we are discussing, where this gift has been flaunted in a fleshly or unseemly manner that has been uncomfortable and even downright scary to those looking on.

I do not know, dear reader, where you would place yourself upon this broad line of thinking regarding the *gift of speaking in tongues*. I hope and pray that wherever you find yourself sitting on this spectrum, you will examine the following verses with fresh eyes and an open heart and mind.

Looking back to the previous chapter, let's review some of the experiences recorded in the **Book of Acts**. Please feel free to look at your notes if you don't want to take the time to turn to every passage. As you review these scriptures, please observe and record what happened when believers had a second experience with the Holy Spirit other than at their initial point of salvation:

Acts 2:1-21

_____

Acts 9:17

_____

Acts 10:44-48

_____

Acts 19:1-7

_____

Paul takes significant measures in **1 Corinthians 12, 13, and 14** to give practical guidelines for enhancing a believer's knowledge regarding the Holy Spirit's gifts and for their use in an orderly manner. We will discuss these various gifts in later chapters, but for now, we are only studying the _gift of tongues_ or _spiritual language._

Compare **1 Corinthians 14:2-4** and **1 Corinthians 14:10-13**. What appears to be the difference between the two uses of _tongues_ given here?

_____

_____

Yes, there are two arenas for the spiritual _gift of speaking in tongues._ Let's address the insight Paul gives us regarding the private or personal use of spiritual language.

What does Paul say are the blessings of _speaking in tongues_ privately found in **1 Corinthians 14:2, 4, 14**?

_____

_____

_____

Add **verse 15** to the passage listed above and relate what these verses say to you about the private use of the *gift of spiritual language* and how it might benefit your walk with the Lord.

_____

_____

_____

Now, glance at **Ephesians 6:10-20** particularly **verse 18**. In what context is Paul writing about?

_____

_____

How do you think the *gift of spiritual language* might benefit a Christian in this setting?

_____

_____

If the *gift of tongues* brings edification or builds up a believer, do you think God would give the private use of tongues to only a few? _____

Read **1 Corinthians 14:14-15.** What happens when a believer prays in their spiritual language?

_____

Share your thoughts regarding how important Paul's prayer language was to him in a private setting as you read **1 Corinthians 14:18.**

_____

_____

Read Jude 1:20-21. Is this further agreement to the edifying work of praying in the Spirit? Your thoughts?

_____

_____

In conclusion, read **Hebrews 13:8**. Knowing that Jesus is the Baptizer in the Holy Spirit, do you think anything has changed regarding the *gift of tongues* since the early church? _____

What are your conclusions as we finish this study of the *gift of tongues?* Please write any concerns, questions, or thoughts you may have:

_____

_____

_____

_____

_____

———————⑨———————

Dynamis Power...

As we look at the various experiences of the Holy Spirit's overflow through New Testament believers, we see the gift of tongues was often one evidence of Spirit baptism. Nevertheless, it is essential to note that it *was not the only or most important* indication.

Jesus told His disciples to wait for the *dynamis* power of the Holy Spirit before they traveled to the ends of the earth preaching and demonstrating the gospel. On the day of Pentecost, men and women listened to Peter preach because something extraordinary was happening. The disciples spoke in languages that were not personally known to them, displaying the presence and power of God in an individual's life. However, it was Peter's preaching with the anointing of the Spirit that pierced hearts **Acts 2:37**.

The fact that three-thousand men (not including women and children) came to salvation in Christ is the most important event of that wonder-filled day. Just as Jesus had stated in **John 16**, these new believers' hearts were pierced by the message of God's convincing love for them by the power of the Holy Spirit.

Have you ever met someone who was literally ablaze with the love and power of God, yet they did not speak in tongues? Of course, you have! We know that the baptism of the Spirit is essential for kingdom work. However, when you read the testimonies found at the back of this study featuring men and women who have received the baptism in the Holy Spirit, you will see that many did not receive their prayer language until sometime after their second encounter with the Spirit.

I experienced the overflow of the Spirit without even asking. God knew my hungry heart and immersed me in the Spirit's power and love, with someone later pointing me to God's Word to explain what had happened. Yet, I did not receive my spiritual prayer language until some months later.

In reading about Paul's conversion and subsequent prayer with Ananias to receive the Holy Spirit, we are not told whether he spoke in a spiritual language at that time **Acts 9:10-19**. Nevertheless, it is apparent from his writings that the Holy Spirit's gift of tongues was a vital part of his walk with Jesus. We

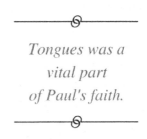

Tongues was a vital part of Paul's faith.

must never have our eyes so much on this gift, as precious and powerful as it is, that we lose the main reason for the overflow of the Spirit in a person's life: the advancement of the gospel and the power to live the Christian life.

Holy Spirit Prayer Language…

Still, the gift of tongues is very evident in the New Testament church, beginning with **Acts 2:4**, stating that *everyone*—all of them—spoke in tongues on the Day of Pentecost. Not just a few or some of them in the upper room. They *all* received this gift.

The controversy the Christian church has faced through the years regarding the gift of speaking in tongues is attributed mainly to two lines of thinking. The first concerns this passage from **1 Corinthians 13:7-8:**

> *Love never fails. But whether there are prophecies, they will fail; whether there are tongues, they will cease; whether there is knowledge, it will vanish away.*
>
> *For we know in part and we prophesy in part.*
>
> *But when that which is perfect has come, then that which is in part will be done away.*

Those who believe that spiritual gifts ended with the first-century church say that the *perfect* mentioned in **verse 8** refers to the completion of the New Testament canon of scripture which took place around the mid or late third century.

However, if you read further in **1 Corinthians 13:11-12**, we find Paul's writing about that which is *in part* or *is partial* passing away. He writes about someday coming *face to face*—implying what is perfect—and *being known just as he is fully known*. That can only refer to his passing into the Lord's *perfect* presence or when Jesus—*the perfect One*—comes again to earth to rule and reign. The same is true for us living today. Each of us will one day see the Perfect One, and we will know Him fully, just as He fully knows us. In the meantime, we still see Jesus as though looking at a mirror dimly while we walk on earth, but one day we will see Him in heaven completely and without hindrance.

The second prevalent line of thinking that disqualifies the Holy Spirit's supernatural gifts is the Corinthian church's confusion and chaos, which Paul addresses in **1 Corinthians 14** (I encourage you to read this chapter entirely). However, that is a shame. Even a simple cursory reading of this passage reveals that Paul is *not* telling that group of believers to quench the Holy Spirit's moving in their midst. Instead, he gives them a concise and orderly way to conduct their meetings so that no gift of the Spirit is missed!

It is in **1 Corinthians 14** that we learn there are two distinct gifts of tongues. One for the *personal benefit* of an individual believer and the other use of spiritual language in a group setting with the *accompanying gift of interpretation*. We will discuss the latter use of tongues in a coming chapter of our study.

The issue in the Corinthian church was the confusion of several people speaking *loudly* in their *personal* prayer language with no interpretation. Their speaking brought a bit of chaos, with no one being able to hear one another. If someone gave a prophetic word or a tongue with interpretation in the group's common language, it was being missed in the din of noise. In other words, Paul said that consideration for the whole group's edification should precede that of an individual.

The Benefits of this Wondrous Gift...

Paul doesn't tell the church never to speak in tongues in their meetings. Instead, he instructs the Corinthian church—and us—that the personal gift of tongues is incredibly beneficial and encouraging in private use. Paul states that he spoke in tongues more than any of the Corinthians in his private conversations with the Lord Jesus.

> *For he who speaks in a tongue does not speak to men but to God, for no one understands him; however, in the spirit he speaks **mysteries**.*

> *He who speaks in a tongue edifies himself, but he who prophesies **edifies** the church.*
> **1 Corinthians 14:2, 4** (emphasis added)

Let's take a look at these two words in bold above in the original Greek.

Mysterion Greek—Meaning: *A hidden thing, a secret, a mystery. Not obvious to the understanding, a hidden purpose, or counsel.*

Oikodomeo Greek—Meaning: *To build, build up, restore, repair, edify, or strengthen. To establish, promote growth, embolden, or encourage.*

The Holy Spirit is directly praying through us.

The gift of speaking in tongues is the ability of the Holy Spirit—who indwells and has made alive a believer's spirit—to pray or communicate things to God that the believer wouldn't know or understand to pray with their natural understanding. It is the Holy Spirit directly speaking to the throne room secrets or mysteries that only the Spirit knows.

In doing so, this language also builds up, encourages, and emboldens our praying in several ways:

- Encouraging us that our spirit is communing with God unhindered. **1 Corinthians 14:2**
- Enhancing and expanding our worship of God. **Acts 2:11**
- It can be a weapon of battle in spiritual warfare. **Ephesians 6:18**
- It builds us up spiritually in ways that surpass our understanding. **1 Corinthians 14:14**
- It supernaturally builds our faith. **Jude 1:20-21**
- The Holy Spirit can prompt us to pray in our spiritual language for reasons we would not have thought about or known to pray for on our own. **1 Corinthians 14:2**

Based on personal experience, other edifying factors of spiritual language are:

- The release of the Holy Spirit bringing felt comfort, peace, joy, or wisdom in confusing, tense, tragic, or fearful situations.

- Heightened awareness of the other spiritual gifts.
- Unlocking areas of the human soul—mind, emotions, personality, and intellect—held captive to the enemy.
- Enabling and expanding our prayer life beyond what is naturally known about a person or situation.

Pastor Jack Hayford describes a time of personal refreshing through praying and worshipping in tongues in his classic book on our subject, *The Beauty of Spiritual Language:*

> *I remember a season sometime back involving an overwhelmingly strenuous schedule. One evening during this time, I stood among the worshipers in a church service where I was to speak. I felt bone weary and mentally numb, stressed by the demands of duty. As I tried to consciously measure what I thought my physical and spiritual resources were for the message I was to bring, I nearly wept...*

> *[However], I was prompted By God's Word to draw by faith upon the potential within the spiritual language to edify myself. So, while the congregation was singing, I stood unobtrusively in the front row...I took the entirety of the time worshiping with my spiritual language...to anyone else I would only have appeared to be singing with the congregation.*

> *But minute by minute, as I sang with the spirit, I became conscious of a steady increase of strength and refreshing within my whole being. My physical frame, my mental mindset, and my spiritual preparedness were all refurbished marvelously. My sudden transformation was characterized ...by **Isaiah 28:12**, the same prophetic context from which Paul quotes regarding spiritual language in **1 Corinthians 14:21**: "This is the rest with which you may cause the weary to rest,' and 'This is the refreshing."*[1]

Paul states that the primary purpose for the gift of tongues in private use is for direct *communication* and *communion* with God that supersedes or bypasses our mind or understanding **1 Corinthians 14:15**. The gift is not directed toward a person—unless interpreted—so that someone might understand **verse 5**. Instead, the intention of this gift is for *praise and prayer* to God. Because tongues originate from our spirit and not our mind, spiritual language enables us to converse or have communion with God directly without human interference, hindrance, or limitation.[2]

This reality is vital in our worship and prayer lives when it seems we have exhausted all that we can think of to say or if we don't know how to worship or pray effectively to begin with! The Holy Spirit, through our spirit, can speak directly to the Father without our help or hindrance.

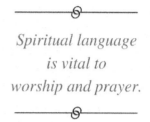

Spiritual language is vital to worship and prayer.

Although the Bible doesn't directly state this, we must note that spiritual language can be started and stopped by the believer. This gift doesn't initiate without the believer's cooperation. Rest assured that in the middle of your workplace or marketplace—out of the blue—the Holy Spirit will not start praying out loud without your consent! **1 Corinthians 14:32**

We find a reference regarding this ability to stop and start prayer in the Spirit in **1 Corinthians 14:26-33**. Paul teaches that the *outward expression* of a person's spirit is subject to that person **verse 33**. A person can choose to be silent, or they can choose to speak. I have never known anyone who couldn't start or stop their spiritual language at will.

There have been countless times I have sensed a prompting from the Holy Spirit to pray in my prayer language. These promptings may come as a tug at the back of my throat or on my heartstrings for no apparent reason. If I was in a public place, I prayed quietly so that no one else could hear me or see my lips move; or I waited to place myself in a more appropriate setting.

Perhaps, when we read about the day of Pentecost, we become concerned that the Spirit just overtook the disciples so that they had no control over their vocal cords. However, in **Acts 2:14**, Peter stopped praying in the Spirit to start preaching. The other disciples likely silenced their prayer languages at that time, at least in an audible way, to listen to Peter and not draw attention away from his message.

Tongues as a Sign...

Another often-asked question is whether a prayer language can be a known language. Yes, that still happens today! My husband, Randy, has spoken in Spanish, Mandarin, and Italian at various times while praying in the Spirit. None of these languages are known to him.

When Randy spoke Spanish, he was praying for a woman's son in a church we were pastoring to be released from the grip of alcoholism. The small group of us in attendance were praying quietly to ourselves in our prayer languages.[3] However, the woman overheard Randy saying clearly in Spanish, *take away the alcohol, take away the alcohol.*

Some years ago, I was in a gathering of young people praying to receive Holy Spirit baptism and their prayer languages. One of the older leaders said gently to a young woman directly behind me, *no, that's not right; you shouldn't speak in a language you know.* The young woman replied, *I have no idea what I am saying; it's my prayer language; I only know English!* That's when the discovery was made that she was speaking a French-Canadian dialect that was the native language of the leader. He interpreted everything she said as various ways of bringing glory and honor to God for His incomparable greatness. For all of us who witnessed this, it was an extraordinary moment of relishing the Lord's presence and power. It is difficult to doubt the reality of Jesus when something like that takes place.

British missionary, Jackie Pullinger, gives several accounts of men and women being delivered completely from horrific addiction through praying in tongues in the memoir of her years in the Walled City of Hong Kong. The British Broadcasting Company (BBC) later verified these accounts in a documentary. Jackie describes her first encounter with this miraculous phenomenon with an addict named Winson:

All you have to do with anyone who has an opium or heroin problem, or any other kind of addiction, is to lock them in a room for a week. Certainly, they suffer agonies during the process of coming off the drug—they may even lose their sanity—but they will also lose their physical dependence. However, the cure does not last; as soon as you unlock the door, they will go straight out to take whatever drug it is to which they are addicted, because their mind and heart continue to crave it...Only Jesus, the Lord of life, can settle a person's heart inside and take away the craving.

I told Winson this many times...[but] he would never condescend to come in [to Jackie's outreach teen center] ...Then one night...I said, "Now, how about you coming inside and praising God." "Okay," he said without hesitation.

He was a very tough Triad [his gang] indeed. And yet here he was standing inside my club praising God at the top of his voice. Then he began praying in Chinese...I have never listened to such a joyous prayer...

It was an extraordinary session, for the next moment Winson began praising God in a new language. This was even more surprising, as he had never heard about the gift from me, nor to my knowledge had he heard anyone else speaking in tongues. After about half an hour, he stopped. The miracle had taken place; he and I knew that he was completely cured of his drug addiction. He had come through withdrawal as he prayed.[4]

Jackie then relates Winson's return to his gang to testify of Jesus and of many others who were set free from addiction with the aid of the gift of spiritual language.

Paul also writes about the Holy Spirit's gift of tongues as a heavenly language *unknown* to man:

> *Though I speak with the tongues of men **and of angels**, but have not love, I have become sounding brass or a clanging cymbal.*
> **1 Corinthians 13:1** (emphasis, mine)

I know of some who have *Googled* words from their prayer languages with amazing results. However, we must not become so preoccupied with the words we are saying instead of leaning our hearts toward what the Holy Spirit is doing at that moment. We can enjoy the beauty and mystery of our words of prayer, opening the door to His presence without knowing the meaning of the words.

Let's enjoy the beauty of spiritual language.

A Gift for Every Believer...

> *Jesus Christ is the same yesterday, today, and forever.*
> **Hebrews 13:8**

We also read that the four gospels each proclaim Jesus is the Baptizer in the Holy Spirit. Because He is the same *yesterday, today, and forever,* we can safely assume that He still holds that role of Baptizer in the Spirit today. Jesus told the disciples it would be to their advantage when he sent the Holy Spirit after His resurrection. One of these advantages is the ability to fellowship and commune directly with God through a spiritual prayer language **John 16:7.**

> *I wish that you **all** spoke with tongues...*
> **1 Corinthians 14:5** (emphasis added)

Paul also writes of his desire for every individual to receive their prayer language and incorporate it often in their private devotion and prayers to the Lord. I believe this gift and all of the Holy Spirit's gifts are available for everyone who comes to faith in Christ, not just a select few. Yes, this is a matter of subjective biblical interpretation. However, God is not partial to some of His children over others, distributing beneficial gifts to an elite group when we all need their aid **James 3:17**.

*And these signs will **follow those who believe***:
In My name they will cast out demons;
they will speak with new tongues.
Mark 16:17 (emphasis added)

We find this passage in a string of promises for Jesus' followers **Matthew 16:9-20**. Some scholars question the integrity of these verses because they are not found in some of the earliest manuscripts. However, the earliest translations, such as the Latin, Syriac, and Coptic, include them. Recognized and highly regarded Christian theologians from the second century, such as Justin Martyr, Tatian, and Irenaeus, give credence to the passages' inclusion in the biblical canon. These admired church leaders supported this text several years after the decease of the first disciples, validating that spiritual language was still alive and well past the early church.

In conclusion, I pray that as you ponder this chapter's scriptures and observations, you will remain open to the possibility that the Lord desires to enhance your communication with Him by releasing the gift of spiritual language into your life.

Let's move forward...

---

[1] Jack Hayford, Litt.D., *The Beauty of Spiritual Language: My Journey Toward the Heart of God* (Dallas, TX; Word Publishing, 1992), page 136.

[2] Dateline: **Speaking in Tongues Medical Study Proves Holy Spirit Praying**, Penn State Research. 2009, https://www.youtube.com/watch?v=NZbQBajYnEc&t=4s

[3] I believe prayer in tongues is acceptable in a group setting when it is done in an orderly manner and if all those present understand what is taking place. Indirectly, Paul calls those who have an understanding of spiritual gifts as *informed* **1 Corinthians 14:23 NKJV**. The Corinthian church got into trouble when folks were praying so loudly in their private prayer language that not only were prophetic words lost in the din of noise, but unbelievers walking into the meeting were potentially put off from receiving the gospel's message, because they couldn't hear the tongues clearly. However, there are many accounts that have been recorded (Pastor Jack Hayford in his book, *The Beauty of Spiritual Language* records a few), where an unbeliever encountered God as someone was praying in tongues in a known language to the unbelieving person.

[4] Jackie Pullinger, *Chasing the Dragon: One Women's Struggle Against the Darkness of Hong Kong's Drug Dens* (Minneapolis, MN; Chosen, a division of Baker Publishing, 2014), pages 84-86.

Study Questions:

- What spoke to you most from this chapter?

- Have you ever had hesitation about receiving the biblical *gift of tongues?* Share your thoughts.

- From the two bullet point lists of blessings regarding spiritual language on *pages 80-81,* which one could you most benefit from right now and why?

- Paul tells us that using our spiritual language builds up and encourages a believer. Share some reasons why you think this happens.

- After studying God's Word and reading this study chapter, has your opinion about speaking in tongues for yourself changed in any way?

7

Receiving
the Gift that
Keeps on Giving

We have briefly examined the Scriptures for a small glimpse of who the Holy Spirit is. Now, we'll suspend our study for this chapter, extending an invitation for you to come to the Lord Jesus as the Baptizer of the Holy Spirit or to aid you as you pray for others for His overflow. I encourage you to first read this chapter through completely.

A Unique Experience Just for You...

After praying for hundreds of individuals to receive Holy Spirit baptism, I now realize that many people have already experienced Him in this manner. However, they often didn't know what had occurred or were unaware of His gifts, including a new spiritual prayer language. Frequently, this overflow of the Spirit happened when the person came to a point of surrendering to the Lord. They may have sensed a physical warmth in their being, a feeling of peace, or an awareness of God's nearness, but they didn't understand what was happening.

I know this is true because of my own experience with Spirit baptism. I had a powerful physical sense of His overflow, but I did not speak in a spiritual language until six months later. A more mature Christian explained the Scriptures to me regarding what had taken place.

On the other hand, many who have asked to receive the Spirit's overflow have doubted their experience because they either didn't have any physical sensation or they didn't receive their spiritual gift of prayer language at that time. Nonetheless, they most likely received His empowerment.

Missionary Jackie Pullinger writes of her experience with Spirit baptism and speaking in tongues:

> *As soon as I made the conscious effort to open my mouth, I found that I could speak freely in a language I had never learned. It was a beautiful articulate tongue, soft and coherent in that there was a clear speech pattern with modulated rise and fall. I was never in any doubt that I had received the sign that I had asked for. But there was no accompanying exultation. I had imagined being lifted up into praise and glory, but it was a most unemotional experience.[1]*

How to Receive? By Faith...

How do we receive the Spirit's overflow? By simply asking for it as Jesus tells us:

> *If a son asks for bread from any father among you, will he give him a stone? Or if he asks for a fish, will he give him a serpent instead of a fish?*
>
> *Or if he asks for an egg, will he offer him a scorpion?*
>
> *If you then being evil, know how to give good gifts to your children, How much more, will your heavenly Father give the Holy Spirit to those who ask Him!*
> **Luke 11:11-13**

We must take Jesus' words here at face value. Just as we receive Him into our lives by faith, we also welcome the Holy Spirit's second experience

90

by faith **John 1:12, 3:16**.

A person at the point of their salvation may have had a physical or emotional response, or maybe they felt nothing at all, and the same is true for receiving Spirit baptism. We receive His work and gifts in our lives *by faith*, whether we have an experience or not. If we don't initially have a physical response, it will come later as we learn to cultivate and nurture God's presence in our times alone with Him.

The Lord will meet you in a way that is special and meaningful to you. We are not *cookie-cutter* objects of His incredible love. At the end of this book, you will have the immense pleasure of reading personal experiences from men and women from diverse backgrounds regarding Spirit baptism. Although I pray their testimonies will encourage you, your experience with the Holy Spirit will be a unique and special moment between You and the Lord. Testimonies should encourage our faith but not become formulas.

I was once taught that a Christian had to have all his *ducks in a row* and have their life squeaky clean before receiving Holy Spirit baptism. However, that is not the truth of the Bible. We come because *we cannot* get our lives squeaky clean on our own, and we need all the power and aid He can give us. We simply come to our Father as we did at salvation and ask to experience this blessing just as Jesus told us to do.

We simply come to our Father and ask...

Find a quiet place where you will not be interrupted for several minutes. Draw your heart close to the Lord Jesus in worship and adoration. It is helpful to speak words of praise quietly *out loud,* even if it is a whisper, to better aid your focus upon Him. Vocalizing out loud will also help you later *if* you seek to receive your prayer language because you will already be in a place of speaking.

With the help of the Holy Spirit—He wants this more for you than you do—focus your thoughts upon the Lord's loveliness and beauty. Reread the previous passage from **Luke 11:11-13** to encourage your faith.

When you are ready, expectantly ask your Heavenly Father for the baptism in the Holy Spirit.

As you continue to whisper your praise and receive the overflow of the Spirit, enjoy the quiet of the moment and the lavishness of His presence. Keep your mind and heart fixed upon Him. Even if your faith seems weak to you, it is enough for Jesus! You may sense peacefulness or joy welling up in the innermost part of you. You may have an awareness of warmth pervading you or enveloping you. There is no prescribed experience. What is happening is exactly how He has meant for it to be. Again, *you may feel nothing*—a rush of emotions or feelings may come later. Nevertheless, you have asked the Lord Jesus to immerse you in His Spirit, which is what He is doing based on His Word.

Now, continue to thank Him *with your voice* for the wondrous Gift He has given you!

> *For all the promises of God in Him are Yes, and in Him Amen,*
> *to the glory of God through us.*
> **2 Corinthians 1:20**

Receiving Your Prayer Language...

Would you like to receive the Holy Spirit's language? There should be no guilt or embarrassment if you are not ready or you don't want to receive it, and most definitely, do not feel pressured. However, if you desire to receive this gift once again, you simply *ask Him* for it. Quite literally, say out loud in your own words something like, *Lord, I desire to speak in tongues*. Next, begin talking *out loud as you make an initial sound or syllable unknown to you*. Just as you were already voicing words of praise, now the Holy Spirit will give you a new vocabulary *as you speak out loud your new language.* Yes, He will do this. Your voice doesn't have to be loud, just loud enough for you to hear yourself.

It is imperative that you *speak out loud.* I cannot stress this enough. The Spirit within you desires to pray through you, and you are giving Him your voice.

What you are doing is similar to Peter's experience of faith when he desired to walk on water, just as Jesus was doing **in Matthew 14:22-31**. In response to Peter, the Lord asked him to step out of the boat and walk on water with Him. Jesus didn't yank Peter out of the vessel. *Peter had to take the first step and swing his leg over the side of the boat.* Similarly, the Holy Spirit won't grab your tongue and make you talk. Instead, you are cooperating with the Holy Spirit by taking the first step as you begin to speak out syllables or phrases you do not know or understand. The Holy Spirit will rise up with His words, and *He will* take over! Yes, really!

There have only been a few times where I have encountered the Holy Spirit taking over someone's tongue without their first surrendering their voice to Him, just like the first disciples on the Day of Pentecost. However, the person was so delighted that the Holy Spirit was praying through them; they were not offended, surprised, or frightened. Almost always, there has been an initial surrender of the person's voice to the Holy Spirit, and as they spoke, He took over their words.

I recall one notable occurrence of the above when a friend and I were ministering at a women's home gathering. As we prayed for a woman sitting on a couch for Spirit baptism and prayer language, another woman sitting at her feet on the floor spontaneously started speaking in tongues. The Holy Spirit had literally splashed down upon her. We all sensed that, and the woman seated on the floor was utterly and completely thrilled.

If you start to voice unknown words but seem to freeze up, either repeat what you first spoke or any type of syllable that is not English or a known language to you. *You are swinging your leg over the boat, just like Peter.*

This is an excellent point of surrender. You have already surrendered your life to Jesus; now, you are reasonably surrendering your tongue to Him. Your words can be a simple consonant and vowel combination and may seem slow and halting. However, simply speak them out and keep going; the Holy Spirit is giving you His new language, no matter if it seems like just a word or two or an entire language.

...swing your 'leg' over the boat.

Keep your mind focused on the Lord and not on what you are saying. Relax and go with the Holy Spirit's flow through you. Your words may have a fast-paced staccato sound coming out in a breathy rush, which often happens. However, *you do* have the control to slow down your speech if you want to. Nevertheless, the Spirit may have a lot He wants to say through you at a fast pace, so don't quench His working!

You may have *thoughts* of unknown syllables––speak out what you are thinking. Regardless, the Holy Spirit has answered your prayer, and He is praying through you! Don't let your intellect or understanding rob you of this great gift. The learned and intellectual apostle Paul didn't **1 Corinthians 13-15, 18**.

Pastor Jack Hayford writes about his initial encounter with Spirit baptism and prayer language:

> *The message had been clear: Receive by faith. And that is exactly what I did. I prayed, "Lord, I ask you to fill me with the Holy Spirit. I want to receive Your power and Your love so I can fulfill whatever You want to do with my life."*
>
> *What took place next happened so quickly it surprised me.*
>
> *As soon as I spoke those words, a phrase instantly came to my mind. It was as clear in my mind as if someone had whispered,*

"I praise You, Lord," but it wasn't a phrase in English. It was four syllables I had never learned (and later, when I mused over them, I knew I hadn't heard them before either). I can still remember them today; in fact, I could write them here, phonetically, except it would seem inappropriate to do so.[2]

At this point of Spirit baptism prayer, almost everyone starts to doubt, thinking—*I am making this up!* However, this is not the case. By *faith*, you have received Holy Spirit baptism and His gift of spiritual language, just as His Word tells us.

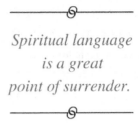

Spiritual language is a great point of surrender.

On the day of Pentecost, the early disciples *began to speak*, and then the Spirit gave them the words. The same is true for us.

And they were all filled with the Holy Spirit and began to speak with other tongues, as the Spirit gave them utterance.
Acts 2:4

Once again, this is an excellent point of surrender. You are trusting the Lord that He has baptized you in the Holy Spirit according to His Word. You are surrendering your voice to the Lord. You are also offering your thoughts to Him by not trying to analyze your new language.

If you try to get a handle on what you are doing in these early stages of your new vocabulary, you might not continue. Paul told us that our prayer language is beyond our understanding, so don't even try to figure it out **1 Corinthians 14:14**. This is a spiritual gift, not a natural one. Keep going.

The new language you are enjoying is the Holy Spirit speaking directly to heaven's throne room, worshiping and praising God, and enhancing your prayer life beyond measure. Don't be concerned if you only have a few words or you seem to be repeating the same words; it is still the Holy Spirit praying through you. The more you keep your mind and heart fixed on Jesus and not over-thinking what is happening, the easier it will be. You will relax as time progresses, and your spiritual vocabulary will grow by the Holy Spirit's initiative, not yours.

You can stop and start your prayer language at any time, and it will never leave you. Receiving this gift from the Lord will strengthen you in any situation. What comfort and strength! Having your spiritual language is a huge benefit and aid to silencing the enemy, positioning you to hear the Lord's voice for discernment or what He wants to do, and the ability to pray or worship when you are not sure what to ask or say. Remember...

> *For he who speaks in a tongue does not speak to men*
> *but to God, for no one understands him; however, in*
> *the spirit he speaks mysteries...He who speaks in a*
> *tongue edifies himself...*
> **1 Corinthians 14:2,4**

Daily Overflow...

Please do not make the mistake I made for years of thinking that this beautiful overflow of God's Spirit is a one-time event. The Holy Spirit desires for us to encounter Him again and again, every day of our lives as we will discuss further in *Chapter 12* of our study. Paul wrote:

> *And do not be drunk with wine, in which is dissipation;* ***but be***
> ***filled with the Spirit.***
> **Ephesians 5:18** (emphasis added)

Let's break down this important verse. The original Greek tense (present-perfect), in the last clause of this verse, means *to be being filled*. In other words, keep being filled continually, just like an eternal pitcher of His living water splashing into and through your spirit.

Consider the original Greek word for the word *filled,* as mentioned in the passage above:

Pleroo Greek—Meaning: *To be filled to the full, to cause to abound, or to be liberally supplied so that nothing is lacking. To have a full measure, be complete, to render perfect, accomplish, and to carry out.*

Paul's use of the word *wine* in this passage *is* literal yet may be considered a summary of anything we allow to *influence* our lives that diverts our attention excessively and keeps us from God's fullness. That could be any variety of things, such as social media, careers, education, money, or relationships. All these are good pursuits in themselves; however, nothing will satisfy our lives as He does.

The word *dissipation* in **Ephesians 5:18** refers to a *watering down* effect, meaning anything that we allow ourselves to come under the influence of other than the Holy Spirit is a cheap substitute. Paul is emphatically stating that nothing compares to being filled with the Holy Spirit. No artificial *high* can come close to the presence of the Most High in our lives.

Walk in the Spirit and you shall not fulfill the lust of the flesh.
Galatians 5:16

Let's invite the tide of the Spirit to flow through us.

Our walk in the Spirit, one foot in front of the other, is the gateway to freedom from hurtful behaviors, either to ourselves or others. Think of our innermost person as being filled with *rivers of living water,* continually refining, cleansing, purifying, and bringing refreshment to us and those around us. There are not many things that can stand in the path of a mighty river's current. The boulders of the enemy's strongholds and our own flesh cannot last long when the tide of the Spirit is flowing through us and eroding the bondages of life that have held us.

First and foremost, God promises Holy Spirit baptism to Jesus' followers for strength, courage, wisdom, supernatural ability, and giftings to preach His thirst-quenching gospel to the world. You will discover greater discernment and sensitivity to what the Lord desires to work through you to reach others. And yet, the Spirit's power and gifts are for your benefit, too, a powerful tool in drawing closer to the Lord Jesus Christ.

Once again, let's read...

Now on the final and most important day of the Feast, Jesus stood, and He cried in a loud voice, If any man is thirsty, let him come to Me and drink!

He who believes in Me [who cleaves to and trusts in and relies on Me] as the Scripture has said, From his innermost being shall flow [continuously] springs and rivers of living water.

But He was speaking here of the Spirit, Whom those who believed (trusted, had faith) in Him were afterward to receive. For the [Holy] Spirit had not yet been given, because Jesus was not yet glorified (raised to honor).
John 7:37-39 AMPC

[1] Jackie Pullinger, *Chasing the Dragon: One Women's Struggle Against the Darkness of Hong Kong's Drug Dens* (Minneapolis, MN; Chosen, a division of Baker Publishing, 2014), pages 62.

[2] Jack Hayford, Litt.D., *The Beauty of Spiritual Language: My Journey Toward the Heart of God* (Dallas, TX; Word Publishing, 1992), page 43.

Study Questions:

• What spoke to you most from this chapter?

• Reread **Luke 11:11-13** on *page 90*. How is your faith is encouraged by Jesus' words?

• Was the reminder of when Peter walked upon the water by taking the first step helpful to you regarding speaking in tongues? Explain.

• Looking at **Ephesians 5:18** on *page 97*, did some things come to your mind that influence your life other than the Spirit? What are they?

• What are your thoughts as we learn that we genuinely can walk daily in the Spirit's overflow?

8
God's
Toolbox

Jesus has given us a toolbox.

Hmmm…I wonder what that means? I can't seem to find the word *toolbox* in my Bible's concordance. However, I often hear my husband use this phrase when referring to the gifts of the Holy Spirit. A toolbox is a good picture of the beautiful source of help that various tools bring when they are collected in one place. When something breaks down around our home, it is so much easier to repair the item when we use the appropriate tool for the job. Have you ever tried fixing a coffeepot with a saw? A toilet with a blowtorch? Or a dishwasher with a hammer?

The gifts of the Holy Spirit are much the same. However, these spiritual *gifts* or *graces* (both of these words are definitions of the same Greek word, *charisma*) do not deal with the mundane aspects of household repair. He provides them to heal and repair the wreckage of human hearts, minds, and bodies for which there is no comparison. Yes, we get annoyed when the sink backs up, but what about the impact trauma, calamity, addictions, failings, betrayals, assaults, disease, and illness have on the human race? People's lives are on the line; their eternal destinies are at stake.

We need help beyond our own finite thinking or power, and the Lord Jesus has equipped us through the Holy Spirit. We have the joyful task of not only taking His good news to the world but demonstrating it.

Before we delve into these supernatural gifts, look once again at **John 16:13-15**. One of the primary assignments of the Holy Spirit is to lead us into God's truth and reveal Jesus to us and through us. How might the Holy Spirit's supernatural gifts reveal God to others as we walk in His gifts?

_____

_____

Read **Mark 16:20** and read **1 Corinthians 12:4-7**. What do you learn as you read about the early disciples, their powerful ministry, and the Holy Spirit's gifts? How might appropriating these gifts affect the way you share the gospel with others?

_____

_____

_____

Let's take a look at the gifts of the Spirit that Paul gives us in **1 Corinthians 12:7-11**. List these nine gifts:

1. _____

2. _____

3. _____

4. _____

5. _____

6. _____

7. _____

8. _____

9. _____

The gifts of the Spirit fall into three areas of service, which helps us better understand them and how they complement each other. Using the list above, try to determine what gift would best fit the categories listed below:

Discerning Gifts – *The Ability to Know:*

- _____
- _____
- _____

Dynamic Gifts – *The Ability to Do:*

- _____
- _____
- _____

Declarative Gifts – *The Ability to Speak:*

- _____
- _____
- _____

In the coming three chapters, we will take each of these spiritual gift classifications and study them individually. However, before we go further in this topic, let's examine our motivation for desiring to have the Holy Spirit dispense His gifts through us. Please read all of **1 Corinthians 13**. Reread **verses 1-3**. What do you think Paul is communicating here?

_____

_____

Let's examine the Greek word *agape* used to express God's unconditional love throughout the New Testament, particularly in this Corinthian passage.

Agape Greek—meaning: *Love, esteem, cherish, favor, honor, respect, accept, prize, relish, and to be devoted to. Unconditional love, love by choice, and an act of the will. Agape denotes an undefeatable benevolence and unconquerable goodwill.*[1] *Agape* never seeks anything but the highest good for the person that its ardent affection is directed toward. This love is not based on chemistry, an affinity, or a feeling. *Agape* is a word virtually unknown to writers outside of the New Testament.

Choose a word or two or a phrase from agape's definition above that encourages your heart. Explain.

_____

_____

_____

_____

Now see **verses 4-8** for a list of love's attributes. Write down these facets of God's *agape* love. Maybe look at various Bible versions to see how they define these attributes from the original Greek into English. A Bible app on your phone will be helpful here (i.e., YouVersion, Bible Gateway).

	1st Translation	2nd Translation	3rd Translation
•			
•			
•			
•			
•			
•			
•			
•			
•			
•			

- _____
- _____
- _____
- _____
- _____
- _____

How do these attributes of God's unconditional love and the love He calls us to demonstrate impact your life?

_____

_____

Why do you think it was imperative for Paul, with the anointing of the Holy Spirit, to place the definition of God's love and how He calls us to live in the midst of his treatise on spiritual gifts?

_____

_____

_____

———————————⑨———————————

God's Toolbox...

Yes, the Lord gives us an amazing *toolbox* filled with the Holy Spirit's extraordinary gifts!

Let's take a look at the Greek word for *gift* Paul uses in **1 Corinthians 12-14**:

Charisma Greek—Meaning: *To show favor, a gift of grace, an undeserved benefit.* It is related to other words derived from the root *char*a, meaning *joy, cheerfulness, and delight*. The suffix, *ma*, indicates the *result of grace*, so *charisma*, is a *gift of grace, a free gift, divine gratuity, a spiritual endowment, or a miraculous faculty*. It is primarily used to designate the gifts of the Spirit.

From the Greek words *charisma, and Pentecost* (which we previously looked at), we find where the designation *charismatic* or *Pentecostal* believers is derived from for those who believe in the gifts and baptism of the Spirit for today. You will also hear this same designation as a type of *church* that believes in the *charisma* of the Holy Spirit past the early church. Once again, there is a broad spectrum of practices from the out-of-order crazy to the almost unseen belief in the Spirit's gifts—preached but not practiced.

Think about all the gifts you enjoy giving in love and generosity. How much more powerful are the Holy Spirit's *charisma* or gifts He offers us out of His inexhaustible, incomparable, and unconditional love?

We must note that we cannot *earn* these spiritual graces. The Spirit bestows them through us for the purpose of displaying God's love in any situation of need. When we dispense a gift of the Spirit, we are providing a gift from Him to the recipient. Because of the joyful root of charisma, *chara*, the intent of  these gifts is not to abuse or harm. They are meant to bring healing, hope, wisdom, encouragement, meet a physical need, or demonstrate God's power—always drawing the recipient closer to Him.

God's toolbox is absolutely free.

Yes, there are occasions when the Holy Spirit will work through one of His gifts to bring correction or rebuke. However, the intent is the same—drawing the person or church closer to Christ. A case in point would be Peter's dealing with Ananias and Sapphira in **Acts 5:1-11**.[2] We read a few verses later in **Acts 5:14** that *believers were increasingly added to the Lord, multitudes of both men and women*.

Jesus told us in **John 16:13-15** that the Spirit would take what is of His (Jesus) and declare it to us. If a supposed gift of the Holy Spirit doesn't *look* like the Lord Jesus and His ministry, as evidenced in the Bible, we should be wary.

In the coming chapters, we will look at the three classifications or categories of spiritual gifts:

- **Discerning:** *Words of Wisdom, Knowledge, and Discerning of Spirits*
- **Dynamic:** *Faith, Healings, and Miracles*
- **Declarative:** *Prophecy, Tongues, and Interpretation*

Paul lists the spiritual gifts in no particular order, possibly so that his readers wouldn't rank the gifts from the greatest to the least. Putting the gifts in a category merely aids us in discovering each of their similarities or characteristics. Although the Old Testament gives several accounts of the Holy Spirit's manifestations, for our study, we will only concentrate on New Testament examples of these graces in our continual prayer to be like the New Testament church.

As we survey the landscape of spiritual gifts through the New Testament, it is sometimes difficult to know which gift is in operation. Often, they overlap one another and work in tandem together.

Paul's adventure at sea is an excellent example of this overlap of supernatural gifts in **Acts 27**. At first glance, is it a prophetic *word* or *message* (we will use these two words interchangeably from now on) that Paul speaks concerning an impending shipwreck? Or is it a word of wisdom or knowledge? We can ask the same question later when Paul receives encouragement from an angel. When Paul acts upon the angel's word, is that a gift of faith? Could it be a gift of miracles? The bottom line to Paul's voyage and shipwreck story is that it doesn't really matter what gift was at work. The outcome was the demonstration of God's power and love rescuing 276 lives!

Yes, the Entire Toolbox...

The purpose for differentiating between the gifts and how the Holy Spirit might use them through us is to open our awareness to their availability. By examining the Scriptures for these gifts, we gain confidence and expectancy that God can use us! It is difficult to use a hammer when a wrench is needed to loosen a bolt. If we know that the wrench is in our toolbox, we will be better positioned to effectively get the job done because we know what a wrench looks like and what it does.

If a person I am ministering to needs guidance in a difficult situation, they probably do not need a gift of healing or miracles because a word of wisdom would be the best gift at that moment.

Paul writes that we should desire the *best gifts* **1 Corinthians 12:31**. Most scholars believe he meant we should expect the *best or the most appropriate gift* to be used in a given situation. From reading all of **1 Corinthians 12, 13,** and **14**, it is clear that every believer has the Holy Spirit's complete toolbox in their lives, meaning a Christian can operate in every gift when led to by the Holy Spirit.

In the full context of these three chapters in Corinthians, the Spirit does not endow us with just one or two gifts for our lifetime, and that's all we get **1 Corinthians 12:7-14**. In Him, we receive the *entire toolbox* **Ephesians 1:3**. Paul is writing the Corinthian church in the context of the Holy Spirit's gifts in a *corporate gathering* where, at that moment, He might only dispense one or two of these spiritual graces through a believer.

Throughout the book of Acts, we see almost all of the gifts displayed through Paul, Peter, and other believers. Again, we are no different from the first-century church. God still uses *peanut-butter jar* Christians like you and me to demonstrate the gifts of the Holy Spirit **2 Corinthians 4:7**. He simply asks that we humbly make ourselves available to pour His gifts through to others.

The gifts or *charisma* of the Spirit are just that—gifts. He gives them as He desires. We must never try to *make up* a gift if we are not genuinely sensing that He is at work. Here lies the dilemma for the earnest believer, especially when we are first trying to find our footing. We sometimes won't be sure if it is the Holy Spirit prompting us or if our thoughts or emotions want to minister on behalf of someone's situation.

These thoughts are a normal reaction for everyone, yet we can't let our fears cause us to limit God's working through us. We learn by stepping out in faith when we sense the Spirit's prompting. And I believe it is never inappropriate to say, *I think this is what the Lord is saying or doing*, providing a disclaimer if we do get it wrong. Whatever we believe the Spirit is prompting us to do, if it is genuinely from Him, it will resonate or confirm its truth to the recipient. More on this subject will come later in our study.

Our total dependence on God keeps us humble and reminds us of Who is in charge. A Christian can and will grow in confidence in sharing the gifts of the Spirit as they step out in faith, but we are still human and can make mistakes. For this reason, we must have a dynamic relationship with the Word of God for ourselves and maintain an intimate relationship with Christ through the Holy Spirit.

> *Our total dependence on God keeps us humble.*

Helpful Tips from God's Word...

Paul gives us sound advice:

> *Do not quench the Spirit.*
> *Do not despise prophecies.*
> *Test all things; hold fast what is good.*
> *Abstain from every form of evil.*
> **1 Thessalonians 5:19-22**

James, the half-brother of Jesus and the pastor of the first-century Jerusalem church, also provides us wisdom in discerning whether something is from God in **James 3:13-18**. For our study of the Holy Spirit's gifts, we can apply this passage as a litmus test to a gift someone is administering:

> *But the wisdom that is from above is first pure, then peaceable, gentle, willing to yield, full of mercy, and good fruits, without partiality and without hypocrisy.*
> **James 3:17**

When we sense the Holy Spirit's desire for us to impart one of His gifts to another person, we should ask ourselves these simple questions:

- Does this word or action line up entirely with the written Scriptures?
- Is this word or action bathed in God's love?
- Will this word or action bring encouragement, edification, or an exhortation in love?
- Am I willing to not give this word or action—yielding to others, the atmosphere of the moment, or to the Holy Spirit?
- Will I be able to proceed with what I'm sensing in a way that won't bring confusion to the situation?

If our answers are *yes* to the above questions, we can take the step of dispensing our gift. If we sense agitation, anger, or any other underlying motivation other than *agape* love, it would be best to hold back what we were going to share, submit it to wise leadership if that is possible, and give the Lord time to tell us what is really going on in our hearts and minds.

Author and teacher Maureen Broderson writes this regarding the Holy Spirit's gifts in our lives while we engage in spiritual warfare:

> *The effective utilization of God's spiritual weapons is most assuredly dependent upon our understanding that our*

*paramount responsibility is to prayerfully inquire of the Holy Spirit for the revelation of His strategy and timing related to their use. The Holy Spirit will faithfully distribute His gifts of faith, wisdom, knowledge, discerning of spirits, and working of miracles as He direct us in the robust implementation of his weapons (see **1 Corinthians 10:7-11**). For a vast number of reasons, the heat of battle in not the time for us to guess or rely on our own understanding; we need the Lord's perspective (see **Proverbs 3:5-6** and **Colossians 1:9**).[3]*

When Paul addresses the Corinthian Church in chapters 12-14 of his letter, he tries to bring order to their corporate meetings. He doesn't want them to stop what they were doing completely. Instead, he desires they continue in a manner that would bless and enhance their meetings in a more significant way. These believers were zealous in their availability to the *charisma* of the Spirit; however, they kept *crossing a line* and missing opportunities for everyone to be encouraged in God's presence.

As we carefully read **1 Corinthians 14:26**, we discover that the Holy Spirit wants to reveal Himself every time we meet:

How is it then, brethren? Whenever you come together, each of you has a psalm, has a teaching, has a tongue, has a revelation, has an interpretation. Let all things be done for edification.

The wonderful exhortation in this verse is that we should all expect to have a spiritual gift to share when we come together with other believers. However, because we fear the same confusing outcome that was evident in the Corinthian church, we tend to enter a meeting with no expectation at all! Let's always contend for spiritual gifts to be present in our times together but always in an orderly, appropriate, authentic, and God-honoring way.

Rev. Dennis Bennett also instructs us:

*The other extreme has been the idea ... [that someone could]...manifest [the gifts of the Spirit] whenever he chooses, sort of an independent "one man band"! While it is true that the gifts reside within Christ in us, yet the Scripture clearly teaches that they are manifested only at the Holy Spirit's discretion 1 **Corinthians 12:11**. God is trying to show us that we need one another, that we can't get along all by ourselves. The body of Christ is made up of many members, and God has purposely planned the release of the gifts "as He wills" so that Christians would need one another in order to function effectively for Him.[4]*

Let's note that the gifts of the Holy Spirit are not to be confused with the *gifts of motivation* or *calling*, as mentioned in **Romans 12:6-8** and **Ephesians 4:11-12**. Studying these gifts from the Father and the Son is exceptionally constructive for knowing what God has wired into the DNA of our individual ministries and life's passions. However, our study here focuses primarily on the Spirit's supernatural toolbox of gifts from which *every* believer can draw, no matter their ministry or calling.

Paul makes no mistake in placing the *Love Chapter*, **1 Corinthians 13**, squarely in the middle of instruction regarding spiritual gifts. The original letter to the Corinthians was not written in chapters, so there is no segmentation in the original manuscript. Paul's letter was one long treatise, full of

Love must motivate our every action.

practical help in moving in the gifts of the Spirit, with God's love being the central message and only motivation for their use.

The Holy Spirit's gifts are not intended to be a badge of spirituality or as a way to validate human pride or ego. We will tread into dangerous waters **Acts 8:9, 14-25** if we seek spiritual gifts for any other purpose than to manifest the agape love of God.

112

Pastor Steve Schell writes:

*A beautiful gift can be spoiled if it's given with a wrong attitude, and that's especially true when it comes to the gifts of the Spirit. Something that was pure and meant to heal, comfort, or bring joy when it was sent from heaven can be delivered in such a way that it does just the opposite. It wounds, disturbs, or leaves someone sad. Whatever comes from God is perfect **James 1:17**, but He delivers His gifts through imperfect people, and that's where trouble can enter in. A human messenger can take a perfect gift and deliver it with anger, fear, or pride. A messenger might "edit" a message by mixing some of God's words with some of their own until that message no longer resembles what God intended; it now says whatever the messenger wanted it to say.*[5]

We should humbly ask ourselves what our motives are before speaking or ministering any gift. I know this from personal experience, both on the giving and receiving end of spiritual gifts that were not expressed in love or were motivated by self-seeking or self-promotion **James 3:13-18**.

As we encounter various situations in our daily lives, let's be encouraged to reach into the Holy Spirit's ministry toolbox. May we desire these spiritual gifts so that God's abounding grace, His matchless glory, and His limitless love have the opportunity to heal, encourage, and edify anyone who needs His touch.

[1] Jack W. Hayford, Sr. Editor, *New Spirit Filled Life Bible*, New King James Version (Nashville, TN: Thomas Nelson, Inc., 2018), *Word Wealth –Agape: Romans 5:5.*

[2] Ibid. A note from the above referenced Bible at **Acts 5:1-11** reads: "Ananias and Sapphira were judged for their hypocrisy and lying to God, not for their decision to retain some of their personal property for themselves (v.4). The severity of the punishment for such a small offense may seem intolerant and graceless (see Luke 9:54-55), but it was necessary both to establish apostolic authority in the early church and to safeguard the church's purity."

[3] Maureen Broderson, *Victorious Spiritual Warfare, So Simple, Grandma Can Do It* (Washington, DC; Vide Press, 2021), page 76.

[4] Rev. Dennis and Rita Bennett, *The Holy Spirit and You: A Study-Guide to the Spirit-Filled Life* (Plainfield, NJ; Logos International, 1971), page 79.

[5] Dr. Steve Schell, *The Promise of the Father: Understanding and Receiving the Baptism with the Holy Spirit* (Federal Way, WA; Life Lessons Publishing, 2020), pages 113-114.

Study Questions:

- What spoke to you most from this chapter?

- What are your thoughts regarding the Holy Spirit's extraordinary toolbox?

- Reread **1 Thessalonians 5:19-22** on *page 109*. What does this passage convey to you?

- From the list of bulleted questions on *page 110*, which one do you think takes top priority and why?

- Share your thoughts about why Paul might have placed his teaching regarding love in the midst of training the church about the Holy Spirit's gifts.

9

Knowing What
You Don't Know

The Discerning Gifts

Have you ever had someone share something with you—even unknowingly to them—that only God could have known about? Because that happened, you were encouraged that He saw and knew you personally?

Have you ever experienced a time when you just didn't know how to proceed or handle a situation? Or perhaps you found yourself in a circumstance, and somehow, deep inside, you knew something was not quite right? Maybe someone was saying all the right things; however, you were experiencing an unsettled feeling, but you weren't sure why?

Each of these scenarios beckons the call for help from the *Discerning Gifts* of the Holy Spirit. Let's take a journey through the New Testament and discover some of the benefits of these precious graces—these *charismas* of the Holy Spirit.

Let's examine a few examples of the *gift of a word of knowledge*. After reading the passages, describe how you think this gift was displayed and what was the resulting outcome:

John 1:47-51

_____

_____

John 4:5-19

_____

_____

Acts 5:1-11

_____

_____

Acts 9:10-12

_____

_____

In your own words, write what your thoughts are regarding the spiritual gift of a _word of knowledge_ and why this gift would be beneficial in a situation:

_____

_____

_____

Now, let's turn in our Bibles to verses that display the gift of a _word of wisdom_. After reading the passages, describe how you think this gift was expressed and what was the resulting outcome:

Matthew 22:15-22

_____

_____

Acts 15:12-22 (James demonstrating this gift)

_____

_____

Acts 27:9-11

_____

_____

In your own words, give your definition of what a _word of wisdom_ is and why this spiritual gift is helpful:

_____

_____

_____

_____

Why do you think a _word of wisdom_ differs from someone's natural wisdom?

_____

_____

Turning now to the gift of _discerning of spirits_, let's visit the passages listed below. Describe how this gift was presented and what the outcome was:

Luke 9:51-56

_____

_____

Luke 11:13-13

_____

_____

Acts 16:16-18

_____

_____

Record what you think the gift of *discerning of spirits* is and why it would be meaningful in a time of need:

_____

_____

_____

———————— ❂ ————————

There are many times throughout our lives we find ourselves absolutely stymied as to how to proceed in a matter. We need more than our natural knowledge, wisdom, and discernment to produce a breakthrough. However, our Father has an infinite vantage point of all-knowing— *omniscience*—that our finite brains can't fathom. The Holy Spirit may give a believer His knowledge or perspective that provides supernatural help when our practical wisdom has hit a brick wall. Although each of these graces can stand alone, they can often work together. Again, it is not crucial to differentiate these gifts, but understanding their distinctives helps us to be aware that the Holy Spirit is at work in our midst.

A Word of Knowledge...

God amazes us with how much He cares.

The gift of a *word of knowledge* can be pretty astounding to both the person imparting it and the person receiving it! Both parties will know that God has spoken because of the miraculous ability the Spirit has given the speaker to know something unknown to them but is known to the listener. We, like Nathaniel **John 1:43-51**, can be quite amazed that God cares so much about us that He would reveal insight about us that is unknown to another person. This gift of the Holy

Spirit grabbed Nathaniel's attention, drawing him to Jesus, and it gets our attention when it is in operation.

On the other hand, *a word of wisdom* is like a silent partner providing someone the ability to know how best to proceed after a word of knowledge. A *word of wisdom* can also work alone to supernaturally guide a person toward the best course of action that otherwise would have been naturally unknown by those benefiting from the gift.

Let's study a *word of knowledge* first.

Webster's Dictionary defines **knowledge** as *the fact or condition of knowing something with familiarity gained through experience or association. The range of one's information or understanding. The act, fact, or state of knowing.*[1]

However, the spiritual gift of a word of knowledge is the ability to know or perceive information that *the giver* wouldn't *naturally know*.

Pastor Dennis Bennett provides us further insight regarding this gift:

> *In looking at this gift, let us first say what it is not. It is not a psychic phenomenon or extrasensory perceptions such as telepathy (the supposed ability to read minds), clairvoyance (the supposed ability to know things that are happening elsewhere), or precognition (the supposed ability to know the future). These "abilities" are forbidden in God's Word (1 Chronicles 10:13, Deuteronomy 18:9-12).*[2]

Reading Pastor Bennett's words may cause us to pause our seeking the Spirit's gifts in our pursuit of contending for God's authentic working! However, that is precisely where the enemy of our souls wants us—to stop pursuing the Holy Spirit's supernatural enablement. Our adversary is the great counterfeiter, making it all the more imperative that we rely upon God's Word and cultivate the Holy Spirit's work in our lives to genuinely see the devil's defeat that Lord Jesus purchased for us on the cross. We then apply that victory to every situation we face in spiritual warfare prayer **John 12:31, Colossians 2:14-15, Hebrews 2:14**.

We see Jesus displaying this gift throughout the gospels **John 1:47-51, Matthew 12:25, Luke 6:8**. Several times within the four accounts, Jesus either *knew* the thoughts of those around Him or He knew the circumstances of their lives.

A classic example occurs when Jesus relates a significant part of a Samaritan woman's history to her, although He has never before encountered her **John 4:5-19**. The point was not to embarrass her but to reveal the root of her incredible thirst for God. She had tried to quench that thirst by looking for love in all the

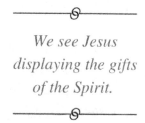

We see Jesus displaying the gifts of the Spirit.

wrong places. Because Jesus states the truth about her without ever speaking to her before, she immediately recognizes that He has extraordinary insight beyond that of natural ability. The Samaritan woman becomes willing to listen to what Jesus has to say.

Personally, when I have witnessed a *word of knowledge*, it has always assured the person that God really did know and care about them, opening doors for further ministry with the person.

The first time I remember the Lord giving me this gift to aid someone took place while praying with an acquaintance whose marriage was in distress. This dear woman was at her wit's end regarding how to save her family.

In my mind, I suddenly had a picture of a chicken coop. I *saw* chickens running and scurrying all over the place, trying to escape their confinement. However, the top of this coop was gone, and when the hens looked upward, they stopped scurrying and realized that the open roof was their way of hope.

I explained to the woman that I was sure I was crazy, but I had this picture for her. She immediately gasped and told me her husband had brought home a cardboard box full of baby chicks just that afternoon. She said that right before our meeting, she had sat on her kitchen floor watching the chicks run crazily all over the box, trying to get out.

She remembered thinking that if those chicks would only *look up*, they would realize their source of rescue. We both knew God was telling her to keep *looking up* to Him alone for the healing of her marriage.

A lovely, poised, and articulate woman came to Randy and me for counsel. According to her, she had told us everything that was troubling her. The Holy Spirit prompted Randy to gently ask her if she had a problem with pornography. She melted into a puddle of tears. She had carried a weight of shame for so many years that she had given up hope for breakthrough in this area of her life. The issue she had initially sought help for seemed to have nothing to do with this addiction. However, a word of knowledge, gently and lovingly spoken, broke the oppression, affecting not only her present circumstances but also revealing the source of many areas of hurt in her life.

Recently, I had the opportunity to pray with someone regarding their ministry. I hadn't met her before, and we hadn't talked prior to our prayer time. However, I *knew*—without any prior natural knowledge—part of her calling was to rescue those ensnared in sex trafficking. When I spoke this to her, the group of women praying around us gasped. They knew that she was in the process of creating a mobile app specifically for that purpose. The Lord was confirming to the young woman to continue with His assignment.

Well, my brothers and sisters, let's summarize. When you meet together, one will sing, another will teach, another will tell some special revelation God has given, one will speak in tongues, and another will interpret what is said. But everything that is done must strengthen all of you.
1 Corinthians 14:26 NLT

From this passage, we see that the Holy Spirit can and will release His gifts in a variety of ways. A person might receive words, a thought, or a *picture* in their mind. Or God may display a charisma in the way He sometimes spoke to some of the Old Testament prophets: by a physical incident that the Holy Spirit makes clear has a spiritual meaning **2 Kings 6:8-11**. Often, a passage of scripture provides the gift of knowledge or wisdom to a person or situation.

At a small women's retreat, the group made time to pray and encourage one another, asking for the Holy Spirit to reign over those moments. Every person prayed for received extraordinary encouragement as those who were seeking the Lord on their behalf made themselves available for Him to work through. Michele was one of the recipients of that special time.

While praying for Michele, I felt led to read:

> *So the King will greatly desire your beauty...*
> *The royal daughter is all glorious with the palace...*
> *She shall be brought to the King in robes of many colors...*
> **Psalm 45:8-15**

Michele writes:

> *Wow, Sue. This brings tears to my eyes. God did do something so awesome for me that night, didn't He? I remember prayer started, and I got up and ran away—do you remember? You and several women hugged me from behind and in front—I was surrounded by love and coaxed back into prayer.*
>
> *These are my notes (still in my Bible): The Lord sees you as beautiful and perfect. Princess, you are royalty. You read **Psalm 45:8-15** and prayed, "We break the spirit of shame and sorrow, in Jesus' Name. Do not give place to thoughts of shame or sorrow. For the weapons of our warfare are not physical, but they are mighty before God for the*

124

*overthrow and destruction of strongholds **2 Corinthians 10:4**.
We lead every thought and purpose away from God captive
into the obedience of Christ." You continued to pray, "Every
thought is captive to Christ. Let the Lord transform your mind
Romans 12:1-2."[3]*

The Holy Spirit used the word *beauty* from **Psalm 45** to pierce Michele's heart because she had never felt beautiful! The Holy Spirit then used the combination of the two words, *beauty* and *shame,* to penetrate the deep places of shame in her heart that even she didn't realize she was carrying from her past. Michele was then irrevocably set free in Jesus' name!

How do we recognize the Spirit's promptings?

How does a person know if the Holy Spirit wants to partner with them to touch someone's life?

As with all the Holy Spirit's gifts, knowing or sensing when He is nudging us to step out of what is natural to us is very subjective. The Spirit speaks to each of us in ways that are unique to our personalities, and in the situations we find ourselves.

When sensing a Holy Spirit nudge, I usually have a thought or *impression* from Him unknown to me prior to the situation. My use of the word *impression* relates that I sense the Lord's presence *pressing* tenderly on my thoughts with words or pictures. I see myself saying or doing something, or a scene plays

*Every spiritual
gift will align
with God's Word.*

itself out in my mind. These impressions are not coming from my *usual train of thought at that moment.* Because of the peaceful sensation my heart is experiencing, and if the thought or picture is in agreement with God's written Word, I can trust more completely that what I'm sensing is from the Lord.

I must also add there are instances when the Holy Spirit wants to dispense a gift through me when I do not feel peaceful! Deep in my heart, words, pictures, or scriptures may resonate that God wants to share something through me. Yet, because I might be in an unfamiliar situation or with people I don't know well—my heart may pound, and I feel nervous! As with anything we desire to grow in and feel comfortable doing, we must keep trying. May I encourage you that when there might be the slightest hint that the Holy Spirit is up to something, let's cooperate with Him!

Recently, I had the opportunity to share at a women's retreat. From the outset of my first teaching session, I sensed that the Lord wanted to do something different from what I had planned. *Yikes!* That was my first response.

Instead of my opening teaching, the Lord nudged my heart to anoint each woman with oil as He gave me words to share with them or pray quietly with them. Although I didn't know any of the retreat participants, they were agreeable to this change of plans, and I followed through. Throughout the remainder of the retreat, many women came to me wondering how I knew many of the specific, personal situations that the Holy Spirit had directed me to say or pray about for them. Because of the events that first evening, the women were very responsive to what the Lord had to share with them for the rest of the retreat weekend.

Sometimes, I think the Lord may be giving me a word of knowledge, wisdom, or a prophetic word (we will learn more about the gift of prophecy in a coming chapter); however, the person I am sharing with isn't responding. When this happens, I usually ask a few more questions to see if the word means anything to them or if the message might mean something else. If what I am sharing truly does not seem to get anywhere, I just let it go and don't press the person. I may have made a mistake, or the timing wasn't right. Regardless, I still try to be faithful to share and learn from the experience.

On this side of heaven, we are still imperfect vessels for His use, but it is still wise for us always to cautiously, courteously, and sensitively proceed with perceived Holy Spirit promptings. Otherwise, we will never learn and make ourselves available for His moving.

Word of Wisdom...

We all want to grow in wisdom. Right?

Webster's Dictionary defines wisdom *as the quality of being wise; the faculty of making the best use of knowledge, experience, and understanding.*[4]

Both believers and unbelievers recognize the need for wisdom. As we mature in age and experience, we are hopefully developing in wisdom as well. However, a Spirit-given *word of wisdom* is a gift of needed insight or direction that transcends what we would consider the natural wisdom of human intellect.

A word of wisdom transcends out natural wisdom.

We see this gift at work throughout Jesus' ministry with how He responds to people, knowing what to do next, and following through with action. His response to the Pharisees' question regarding who should receive taxes is evidence of His divine wisdom. They were attempting to *entangle Him in His talk* **Matthew 22:15-22.** However, Jesus' response of showing them a coin with Caesar's inscription and His answer stopped the religious leaders in their tracks. They could not refute Jesus' wisdom.

I remember a difficult season in our family's life when our eldest daughter tested *the water* of rebellion in her teenage years. I was having difficulty dealing with it; truthfully, I wasn't doing a very good job.

One night, while my husband and I were driving to a sports event, *out of the blue*, the Lord reminded me of an incident with our daughter some years before and my poor reaction. I relived the scene in my mind. With His tenderness and love, I could *see* how the Lord would have handled that particular crisis differently.

When we returned home that evening, we discovered that our daughter had placed herself in a pretty tricky situation while we were gone. Nevertheless, I knew exactly what to do because the Lord had specifically shown me by using the recollection of the earlier incident. The Holy Spirit gave me wisdom on how to handle this incident differently. This incident became a pivotal moment in our relationship at that time. Afterward, I began to wait on the Lord in a more intentional way for how to react to her. For many years now, she has had a personal walk with the Lord, written several Bible studies, and been active in ministry.

The Book of Acts records two incidents where words of wisdom are displayed. In **Acts 13:1-2**, we find the Holy Spirit giving wise direction as to the next steps Paul and Barnabas should take after spending time with the church in Antioch. In **Acts 15:6-22**, the Jerusalem council meets in hopes of gaining a clear understanding of what God would have the new Gentile believers do regarding Hebrew law. The young, predominantly Jewish church faced issues that had never been encountered before. James receives a word of wisdom that resonates as a correct and wise decision with the remainder of the council.

Have you ever had an *aha* moment? Possibly you and others have been hashing out the best course for a given task, and someone has a *light bulb moment* with everyone agreeing that it is the best thing to do. Consider a *word of wisdom* as a *spiritual light bulb* of the Holy Spirit. You suddenly know the best thing to say or do. The evidence of this gift will result in your acting upon the Holy Spirit's voice turning out far better than your natural thinking could have imagined.

A close friend of ours once owned a refrigeration and heating repair business. He had a large account with a fast-food chain, and one of the store's refrigerators broke down during a summer's heat wave. Losing money daily as food spoiled, Rick tried everything from his past experience and training to fix the refrigerator. While praying over the situation, he pictured a small bolt that was very insignificant in the refrigerator's mechanism. Surely, there was no way this tiny metal object could bring down the large freezer! Nevertheless, after another 24-hour cycle of nothing working and still having the same picture in his mind, Rick located the bolt and gave it a twist—voila! He only regretted not responding sooner to what the Holy Spirit had told him.

When we were appointed the pastors of our final church pastorate before retiring, Randy struggled with how to get a men's ministry established. The guys were willing and interested, but Randy's every attempt, such as men's breakfasts, Bible studies, and baseball nights, didn't seem to be getting much traction. Randy was beginning to feel he had run out of options and ideas.

One day when he was out for his power walk, he came to the top of a hill near our home. While standing on the top of that hill, Randy saw the word *summit* in his mind. That moment, he sensed the Holy Spirit prompting him to invite all the men in the church at that time to join him on top of that same hill for a *summit meeting* with the Lord. That is precisely what took place a few weeks later. From that time until our retirement, just over a decade later, the *Men's Institute* of that church bore the fruit of many men coming to Christ, finding breakthroughs in their lives, the power of God's Word to transform, and the overflow of the Holy Spirit.

Discerning of Spirits...

The concluding gift we'll examine in the category of *Gifts of Discernment* is the Holy Spirit's ability to *discern spirits*.

There are three types of spirits at work in the world:

- The human spirit

- Evil spirits or demons
- The Holy Spirit

We must test every spirit.

Discernment is often needed to differentiate which of these three spirits might be at work in a situation. It may seem obvious what the driving force behind a behavior or circumstance might be; nevertheless, that is not always the case. And, if we do conclude that we are dealing with a demonic spirit, we almost always need supernatural ability to discern what type of spirit is presenting itself before us. This gift of discerning spirits can aid us in how to pray and battle in the Holy Spirit effectively.

When Jesus rebukes James and John in **Luke 9:51-56**, He tells them that the *spirit* at work in them is not from Him. Here, Jesus is addressing their human spirit, which, in their indignation, wants to pray for fire to rain down on the Samaritans who won't let Jesus pass through their region. Like these *Sons of Thunder*—Jesus' name for James and John—we sometimes may think that a person or situation is being motivated by the Holy Spirit, but it is just their humanity at work.

I once had the opportunity to pray for a group of approximately thirty women to receive Holy Spirit baptism. The Holy Spirit came and touched each life with His overflow, and all of them received their prayer language. When concluding our prayer time, one woman began exhibiting signs of demonic oppression: talking loudly and physically shaking. She was unable to control herself. Immediately I spoke the authority of Jesus' name to remove the evil spirit. The woman was instantly released, and he returned to her usual self and was so joyful that God had broken her bondage.

In a similar prayer time for Spirit baptism, a woman in the group began to manifest the same type of behavior I previously described. However, in this instance, I sensed it was just the woman's reaction to sensing the overflow, joy, and power of the Holy Spirit for the first time. **Acts 2:13**. I calmly but firmly told her to settle down but continue in her prayer language and delight in the Lord, just not so loudly to disturb or distract others. She complied with no problem at all, overjoyed in the Holy Spirit.

The gift of discerning spirits may present itself by what you sense. Do you suddenly feel ill at ease, confused, or have a sense of heaviness? Possibly, you may suddenly have a word, a picture, or scripture. As with all the Spirit's gifts, we grow in this gift by experience.

A few weeks ago, Randy and I were asked to be the *seasoned* couple to provide prayer support for over 500 middle and high school students, youth leaders, and pastors. Although there seemed to be a heaviness about the worship times, I attributed it to the worship band's choice of music and the vocalists being a little offkey. However, when the camp's overseeing director stepped on the grounds, she felt a sense of opposition from the enemy. Together, we prayed boldly in the name of Jesus outside the building. She then had all the youth leaders walk through the meeting place and pray. Well, a genuine breakthrough happened for hundreds of students that night. Many gave their lives to Jesus, and many, if not hundreds, of those students, experienced Holy Spirit baptism with the evidence of speaking in tongues.

Once while visiting London, two friends and I made our way from Trafalgar Square to Piccadilly to shop for Christmas. We turned a corner. Suddenly I *knew* we needed to get out of there as fast as possible. I stated this to my friends, although I couldn't explain why, except that I had a sense of foreboding. We made it to the nearest corner when all three of us looked up to see that we had landed squarely in the area of London's sex shops. We hadn't noticed where we were, just that sense that we were in a place the Lord didn't want us to be at that time.

You may hear someone saying all the *right words*, but you sense something is not correct. This situation can be very confusing during a ministry time, especially when you know the person you are addressing is a sincere believer. However, Christians and non-Christians alike can say the right Christian words and phrases but still have oppression—*not possession*—in an area of their soul.[5] I often encounter the need for this spiritual gift during pastoral counseling to bring insight I simply don't have. I have experienced this to the degree that licensed marriage and family therapists have requested prayer for greater Holy Spirit discernment for their own lives and clients.

This was the case of Paul and the young woman with a spirit of divination or foretelling the future **Acts 16:16-18**. The slave girl was speaking the truth but was motivated and enabled by an evil spirit oppressing her. The Holy Spirit's gift of discernment enabled Paul to pinpoint what spirit was at work and, in Jesus' name, break the enemy's power over the girl's life, much to the chagrin of her masters.

Some time ago, my friends, Kareen and Eileen, helped me pray for a breakthrough for a young pastor's wife. The woman lacked clarity about her identity. She also had difficulty expressing her emotions, thoughts, and desires, bringing frustration to herself, her marriage, and the church she was serving. While she was talking, Eileen received a *picture* of the woman in her mind from the Holy Spirit. In the picture, the young woman was shaking her hands as if trying to dry them off. Then, she would look heavenward and raise her hands in exasperation. Truthfully, Eileen looked pretty funny demonstrating this! Kareen then piped in, *I saw the same thing too!* Kareen then gave the same demonstration.

These pictures turned out to be gracious *words of knowledge* as the young pastor exclaimed that she had demonstrated those same gestures as recently as the day of our meeting together. These gestures conveyed her frustration with her life and the Lord, saying, *I'm so confused!* The Holy Spirit impressed upon us that a spirit was harassing her with confusion, and we needed to remove it in Jesus' name before we could proceed further in counseling.

I can attest that the young woman experienced breakthroughs on many levels that night. She has grown in confidence in her identity and ability to communicate her ideas and feelings, and she later returned to school to further her education and has a thriving career, marriage, and ministry.

The Gifts of Discernment: *words of knowledge, words of wisdom,* and *discerning of spirits* are tools in our spiritual toolbox that God can use to get to the heart of matters that would otherwise take hours of thought, research, ministry counseling, or would not ever be revealed by human methods. Let's be available and willing to take baby steps and minister in His love when the Lord answers our prayers to be used by the precious and powerful Holy Spirit.

God's toolbox helps us get to the heart of things.

---

[1] https://www.merriam-webster.com/

[2] Dennis and Rita Bennett, *The Holy Spirit and You: A Study-Guide to the Spirit-Filled Life* (Plainfield, NJ; Logos International, 1971), page 158.

[3] Interview update with Michelle Gutierrez, July 2022.

[4] https://www.merriam-webster.com/dictionary/wisdom

[5] For more regarding emotional healing and spiritual breakthrough from lies of the enemy in the realm of our emotions and thoughts, please consider reading, *Refresh: Transformed Thoughts, Emotions, and Lives*, available on Amazon or through my website: www.sueboldt.com/books.

Study Questions:

- What spoke to you most from this chapter?

- Share an experience you may have had with one of the spiritual gifts we just studied.

- Why do you think a *word of knowledge* would be reassuring to someone receiving it?

- What are your thoughts regarding the frailty of human wisdom in light of having God's wisdom?

- Have you ever experienced an uneasiness you couldn't explain at first? As you look back on that incident, could it have been the Holy Spirit's *gift of discernment* at work? Explain.

10
Dynamis
Unleashed

The Dynamic Gifts

We will designate our next group of graces or gifts as the *Dynamic Gifts*. These three gifts are a bit more difficult to differentiate as they genuinely seem to complement and overlap each other in their manifestation. It isn't always easy to know where one gift ends, and another begins. However, we'll look at a few examples of each gift to broaden our understanding.

The first of these spiritual gifts that we will examine is the *gift of faith*. From the outset, the Scriptures are clear that this grace is not to be confused with the faith-life of a believer in everyday decisions involving trusting God with their lives and situations. If that is true, what is the *gift of faith*, and why would the Holy Spirit lavish the gift upon a believer in need?

Examine the passages below and describe why you think the Holy Spirit provided this extraordinary gift and what were the resulting outcomes:

Mark 11:22-24

_____

_____

Acts 3:1-8

_____

_____

Acts 27:21-25

_____

_____

In your own words, write your definition of the _gift of faith_ and why it would be beneficial:

_____

_____

_____

Gifts of healings come next. Notice the plurality of the word used. Why do you think that might be?

_____

_____

_____

Looking at the passages listed below. Describe the action that the Holy Spirit led Jesus or the person praying to take and the resulting outcome:

Luke 4:40

_____

_____

John 9:6-7

_____

_____

Acts 3:1-10

_____

_____

Acts 9:36-42

_____

_____

Acts 20:9-12

_____

_____

In your own words, write your definition of the *gifts of healings* and why they would be helpful in a given instance (I know, this is too obvious!):

_____

_____

_____

The *working of miracles* is the name Paul designates for miracles that are not physical healings. Again, read the passages below. Describe how this gift was demonstrated and what resulted:

Matthew 14:15-21

_____

_____

Luke 5:1-11

_____

_____

Acts 8:39-40

_____

_____

Write your definition of the *gift of working of miracles* and why it would be helpful in time of need:

_____

_____

_____

Why do you think these three gifts are categorized as *Dynamic Gifts* based on the definition of power *(dynamis)* found on *page 24?*

_____

_____

_____

_____

———————⑤———————

The Lord may use these dynamic or power gifts to demonstrate His supernatural ability to work beyond what we consider natural laws. Throughout the Old and New Testaments, God displays His presence in ways that cannot be explained or refuted by the believing and unbelieving alike.

The Gift of Faith...

The *gift of faith* is different from what we think of as *cultivated faith* that we find in the list of the fruits of the Spirit **Galatians 5:22**.

> *It's impossible to please God apart from faith. And why? Because anyone who wants to approach God must believe*

both that he exists and that he cares enough to respond to those who seek him.
Hebrews 11:6 MSG

Everything about our walk with Jesus is based upon our *faith* in who He is, what He has done, His heart of pure agape love, and what He can do. We will not get very far in our journey in Jesus if we are not willing to trust Him for the small and large details of our lives, and no one can do our faith walk for us. *Cultivated faith* is our day-by-day growing faith as we feed upon and are obedient to God's Word. This faith also increases as we act upon the Lord's direction as He speaks to us personally—always aligning with His written Word—and when we are encouraged by the testimonies of other believers when we are in consistent fellowship.

The *gift of faith* differs from our cultivated, *garden-grown* variety, as it is a specially given *unction of grace* to a Christian to believe or know with *certainty* that God will perform a miracle. We constantly face situations where we must choose to believe God by exercising our faith, but a *gift of faith* is purely Spirit-initiated, with no effort on our part.

The gift of faith differs from our cultivated faith.

Donald Gee writes this about the gift of faith:

> *It would seem to come upon certain of God's servants in times of special crisis or opportunity in such mighty power that they are lifted right out of the realm of even natural or ordinary faith in God—and have a divine certainty put with their souls that triumphs over everything.*[1]

We often hear Jesus' words in **Mark 11:22-24** regarding a Christian's faith *to move mountains*. These words are sometimes misquoted to promote a believer's whim or fancy at a given moment which is presumptuous. In the context of the whole of Scripture, we see that the mighty miracles of the

Bible were dependent on a person's faith *after* God's will was first revealed to them.

1 John 5:14-15 clearly tells us that when we pray according to His will, the answer will be a resounding *yes!* However, God, in His sovereignty and love for us, may answer many of our prayers with *no* or *not yet*. He is the perfect Father; far above and beyond how any caring and wonderful human parent loves their children for their maximum benefit and good.

A *gift of faith* differs from normative belief when God is about to do something extraordinary, and His heart desires to involve the partnership of a believer to enjoy a miracle blessing.

If God, not our personal desires, tells us that He wants to move a mountain, *the gift of faith* will provide the certainty in our hearts that He will indeed come through as He said. The *gift of faith* is a charisma of pure joy. It is not born out of a struggle with doubt, repetitive thoughts or words, or trying to will something to happen. Mountains will move if He tells us that is what He is up to and He grants the faith to carry it out!

We see the gift of faith throughout Acts.

Peter demonstrates the gift of faith when he speaks to the lame man at the gate called Beautiful on the temple grounds. **Acts 3:1-8** tell us that the man who couldn't walk from birth had been there daily. Indeed, Peter and John, who was with Peter then, had often passed by the man lying there. Yet, on one particular day, Peter appears to receive faith beyond his nurtured belief in Christ and speaks a healing word to the lame individual in the authority of Jesus' name.

We also see the gift of faith at work in Paul's life when he sails with over two hundred others to Rome, and their voyage appears doomed due to a catastrophic storm. It seems that Paul receives a *gift of faith* after an angel of the Lord appears to him and provides encouragement. Paul knows that everyone on board will make it through when no one else dares to dream that rescue is possible.

> *So keep up your courage, men, for I have faith (complete confidence) in God that it will be exactly as it was told me.*
> **Acts 27:25** AMPC

I recall two times when I believe God granted me a *gift of faith* far exceeding my cultivated trust in Him. The first instance concerns our family's move to plant a church in northern California's technology region. Every aspect of the transition was challenging as if we were jumping off a cliff of security into an unknown abyss. To us and others, there were giants in the *land of technology* regarding a lack of housing and finances that made our transition appear impossible, much like when Israel sent spies into Canaan before receiving their promised inheritance **Numbers 13**.

During a Sunday morning church service, the Lord granted me an extra portion of *faith* to know that everything was going to work out in His timing and plan. Shortly after, several people spoke prophetic words to us, confirming that we were on the right course. God *did* make a way in the wilderness during that time in our lives. He graciously provided for all of our needs and then some. We have shared this story countless times to encourage others to trust the Lord for what He calls them to do.

The second occasion I am confident the Holy Spirit granted me a *gift of faith* was regarding my health. While on a personal retreat, the Holy Spirit directed me to read Isaiah **41:10-13**. I sensed Him telling me from these verses that I was to prepare myself for something challenging that would soon happen. Nevertheless, I was not to fear. Through the passage, the Lord said He would stand with me and defeat my enemies to such a degree that it would be as if they had never existed. This experience was *not* a foreboding premonition but instead was comforting and joy-filled. Little did I know that I would be diagnosed with an extremely rare and medically incurable adrenal cancer two weeks later!

When the cancer returned for the third time, the entire oncology department of the hospital treating me told me I was dying and to get my affairs in order. However, sensing God wasn't done with me yet, I convinced my surgeon to debulk the tumor so I might live a few months longer to see what the Lord would do. The surgeon also told me I was *winding down* after seeing a second scan that confirmed the cancer had metastasized. However, he promised to do his best. Two weeks before surgery, Randy and I experienced overwhelming *gifts of faith* beyond anything we had ever known before or since. I was going to be okay. The Holy Spirit completely removed all fear and worry.

My surgeon told me again I was dying on the day of surgery. Yet, three hours later, he spoke to Randy midway through the operation to say that although he had removed part of my lung, liver, and three other portions of tissue, his team could not find the cancer anywhere, although they could see it on both a CT scan and PET scan!

I have been cancer free for ten years with a fully documented miracle. My enemies truly are non-existent, as the Lord Jesus told me they would be. This cancer story was a five-year journey that I chronicle in *Held in His Hands: A Miracle Story and Encouragement for Your Healing.*[2]

Gifts of Healings...

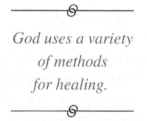

God uses a variety of methods for healing.

Holy Spirit *gifts of healings* minister specifically for the recovery, restoration, and curing of the human body. Notice the plurality of the gift. Each *charisma of healing* stands alone based on the physical healing needed. In other words, God uses a variety of methods to heal folks. He most certainly works through the medical community out of His great love for humanity, and we should not discount that truth. Still, miraculous healing, whether it is over a period of time or in an instant, is needed. Every situation is different, and each healing is a new gift being ministered! Those ministering in this gift must depend on God for each circumstance.

Throughout the Gospels, we find Jesus, and later his disciples in the **Book of Acts**, healing every sort of affliction and using various methods in prayer as the Holy Spirit directed them. At times, the discerning of spirits was necessary to ascertain whether a physical malady was the work of a demon or if it was from natural causes resulting from the broken world we live in **Luke 13:11**. Let's take our cues from the examples given in God's Word. When we encounter someone needing healing prayer, let's be open and available to the Spirit's leading in how to proceed.

Occasionally, there seem to be those with a special ongoing grace of ministering healing in Jesus' Name. Throughout the **Book of Acts**, we see Peter demonstrating the gift of healing to the extent that those who were ill were placed in his pathway so that his shadow might bring healing **Acts 5:15**. Possibly, these believers *have simply been more willing* to step out in faith and pray boldly as the Spirit leads them.

Dr. Leslie Keegel, who has often seen God's miraculous working, especially in his home nation, Sri Lanka, writes:

> *Anointing of the Holy Spirit is given to people to demonstrate God's love and power in accordance with the Bible, not for any self-glory. But you must be willing to step out in it at any time 2 Timothy 4:2.[3]*

We can *all* grow in *all* of the Holy Spirit's gifts by being ready, available, and willing. Our faith grows in every arena as we wait upon the Holy Spirit for His instruction, not moving forward with our own human inclinations. This discernment will grow as we are willing to take baby steps of faith, recognizing we may make a few mistakes along the way, but all the while

We can all grow in all the spiritual gifts.

growing in a greater discernment of the Holy Spirit's promptings **Hebrews 5:14.**

Cindy had a painful and persistent earache. Though in misery, she decided to attend a home group meeting in our church to ask for prayer. Several gathered around Cindy to pray for her, but one woman asked the Lord to show her how she should specifically pray. The woman sensed the Holy Spirit prompting her to ask Cindy if she had been poked in the ear. After pondering the question, Cindy remembered that several weeks earlier, while playing with her kids, she had been stuck in the ear by a toy. Cindy had not related the earlier accident with the earache she was now experiencing due to the time lapse between incidents. However, Cindy's earache was immediately gone as the woman prayed for her.

Our young friend Craig was diagnosed with rheumatoid arthritis. His wife and young family were stunned to learn that his doctor thought paralysis was imminent. Craig's doctor explained that he should change his vocation and prepare for the worst.

At a prayer meeting, believers gathered around Craig to pray for him. A prayer group member sensed that the Holy Spirit might want to pinpoint an area of unforgiveness that Craig might be harboring toward someone. Craig agreed that he was resentful toward someone, confessing his unforgiveness to the Lord and those praying for him. The prayer team boldly spoke a healing prayer over Craig in Jesus' name. From that point forward, every symptom of arthritis diminished in Craig's body until it was gone entirely. Craig's physician documented this miracle with great surprise.

Dr. Leslie Keegel writes about a time when called upon to pray for a dying boy while ministering across town from where he was living in Sri Lanka...

> *Seeing the baby lying on a cot, I immediately made my way over to him, lifting him up, holding his slumped head level to mine.*

"I rebuke sickness, I rebuke disease, I rebuke death in Jesus' name!" And I said it all very loud.

The baby sneezed, then he began to cry. I handed him to the startled mother, Winefreda. Feeling bad that I had wakened a sleeping baby, I apologized to her. "Pastor, he was dead!"

The boy had been dead for several hours, but I didn't know that when I arrived. If I had, I never would have picked him up from the cot. Almost all of the forty-plus people who had witnessed this miracle gave their hearts to Christ after I shared the gospel—nothing like a "raising from the dead" to enhance the evangelism process.[4]

Recently, my dear friend Linda was out for a walk with her friend, Vicki, on a busy street. Suddenly, a pickup truck missed the curve in the road ahead of them. The truck plowed into another car which collided with another vehicle, nearly hitting Linda and Vicki as it came their way. The two women scrambled up an embankment, and Linda spontaneously said out loud, *Jesus, what do You want us to do?*

Without speaking to one another first, Linda ran to the truck, and Vicki made her way to one of the other cars. When Linda reached the truck, the driver appeared lifeless on the passenger side floor. Immediately, Linda began to call on the Lord and speak the name of Jesus to him. Without forethought, Linda intentionally breathed as if she were blowing life into the man through the window. She repeatedly said between breaths, *I speak life to you in Jesus' name!* Within moments, the man coughed and sputtered to life.[5]

Over many years, I have witnessed countless healings, from common colds to cancer, multiple sclerosis, eczema, heart failure, respiratory issues, and broken bones. The Scriptures are clear that every Christian is called upon by the Lord to minister and expect healing when praying for the sick **Mark 16:18, James 5:16**. Yet, there have been many times when complete physical healing doesn't occur until the person reaches heaven. When this happens, our faith in God's love, sovereignty, and comfort is our bedrock of strength.

The Gift of Working of Miracles...

The spiritual gift of *working of miracles* is found in **1 Corinthians 12:10**. The Bible defines the word *workings* as:

Energema Greek—meaning: *A thing wrought, an effective operation, a working.*

And, the Greek word for *miracles*? You guessed it—*dynamis!*

Again, we must depend upon the Lord for every individual situation and need. The gift of *working of miracles* designates those extraordinary events the Lord demonstrates that are other than physical healing. We find scores of these miracles recorded in the Old Testament—notably, the parting of the Red Sea for the Israelites and Daniel surviving in the lion's den.

Miracles are extraordinary events other than healing.

The New Testament records many of Jesus' non-healing miracles, including turning water into wine **John 2:1-12**, walking on water **Mark 6:48**, and feeding the multitudes **Matthew 14:15-21**. In the Book of Acts, miracles continue in the disciples' lives, from an angel opening prison doors for Peter **Acts 5:19** to Philip's transport in the Spirit from one location to another **Acts 8:39**.

In today's world, it seems we don't see many non-healing miracles as in Bible times, but that is not the case!

My husband and I, plus countless others, can testify of the provision of financial resources when our bank accounts were at zero. Reports abound of threatening storms being calmed in the Name of Jesus at events or when weather patterns endangered lives. The multiplying of small amounts of food to feed many is continually on display in regions where food supplies are scarce. The denial of needed passports and international visas by governments at first, then their miraculous approval, also counts as the workings of miracles.

Carol, along with other members of our church, formed a team traveling to the streets of Hollywood and Los Angeles, preaching the gospel during a special outreach event. As they concluded an evening of streetcorner evangelism, a young man, obviously high on a substance, began to charge directly at Carol

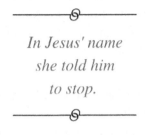

In Jesus' name she told him to stop.

with a knife. In Jesus' name, she told him to stop. The weapon fell out of his hand. The young man picked up the knife and began charging at Carol again. Again, she repeated her command to stop in Jesus' name. It was as if an invisible barrier was protecting Carol and the team. In total, this happened three times within a matter of seconds. The man became so flustered he turned and ran away.

Our mentors and pastors, Jim and Betsey Hayford, share a wonderful story.

Betsey was cooking up one pound of hamburger meat to add to a regular-sized package of spaghetti noodles for her family of five. While cooking, another family of five unexpectedly knocked at their door along with another adult family member. The eleven hungry folks sat down to give thanks for their meal, then Betsey carefully spooned out tiny portions of spaghetti to accommodate everyone. Once around the table, she looked back into the pot she was holding. It was at the level of fulness she had first started with! Betsey once again went around the table, distributing more spaghetti. She dared not look into the pot but couldn't resist. Yes! The pot was still full. She circled the table several times with everyone eating until they were full. And Betsey tells me, the next day, there were leftovers![6]

While driving to a mountain retreat with friends, I forgot about the well-below-empty fuel tank gauge and started up the Sierra Nevada mountains. It wasn't until we were deep into the woods in freezing winter weather, and not one open gas station in sight, that we began to pray. Admittedly, my faith was not very strong as I tried to calculate how long it would take a roadside service to reach us. However, everyone in the car encouraged one another regarding the Lord's faithfulness. We kept rolling along, and rolling along, and rolling along. We rolled right into a gas station after nearly 60 miles of mountain roads, thanking and praising God for this miracle.

Heidi and Rolland Baker encounter the miraculous daily as missionaries to the African nation of Mozambique, where they house and raise thousands of orphans and have started well over 5,000 churches. The Bakers weekly witness the deaf hearing, the blind seeing, and countless other miracles attesting to the power of the Holy Spirit.[7]

One night, while driving street girls back to their homes after an outreach service, men brandishing weapons surrounded Heidi's double-cab truck. The men pinned her vehicle against a cement wall with their three SUVs. One of the men put a gun to her temple as she sat trapped in the driver's seat. Screaming the Name above all Names, *JESUS!* Heidi accelerated onto a curb and drove her large truck, filled with children, through a narrow space between a tree and a lamppost next to the wall. She immediately went to the American Embassy and learned that these same men had just killed four Americans.

The next day, Heidi and Rolland returned to the escape scene and took measurements of Heidi's truck and the space between the tree, lamppost, and wall. There was no possible way that the vehicle could have fit through the much smaller area they measured! Neither the truck, tree, wall, or lamppost had any damage. Heidi laughingly states that she doesn't know if Jesus shrank the vehicle or moved the three barriers. Since that incident, Heidi has miraculously escaped at least five separate death threats upon her life![8]

Randy was leading a home Bible study when a woman requested prayer for her unbelieving husband. She was distraught because her husband had just returned from a business trip abroad, bringing with him various religious stone idols and two paintings depicting false religious characters. The woman was deeply distressed about having these items in her home yet knowing her husband would be angry if she did anything with them.

In Jesus' name, the group rebuked the demonic spirits the idols and paintings represented. When the woman returned home that evening, the stone figurines had fallen off their settings and smashed on the floor. The two pieces of artwork had also fallen off the walls. No one was in the house at the time, and there was no evidence of a robbery. The religious articles were the only items broken in the home.

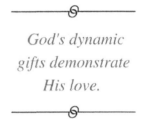

The Holy Spirit's dynamic gifts demonstrate God's love and might to unbelievers and aid His followers when in need. They are not displayed for selfish gain or self-promotion but to bring fame and glory to the One to whom all praise is due. *Truly ours is an awesome God!*

God's dynamic gifts demonstrate His love.

---

[1] Donald Gee, *Spiritual Gifts in the Work of the Ministry Today* (Springfield, MO; Gospel Publishing House, 1963), page 65.

[2] Available on Amazon.

[3] Dr. Leslie Keegel with Robert Hunt, *The Spirit of the Lord is Upon Us* (Anaheim, CA; Foursquare Missions Press, 2017), page 31.

[4] Ibid, page 82.

[5] Firsthand account from Linda Stanley, November 19, 2022. Used with permission.

[6] Firsthand account from Betsey Hayford, August 5, 2022. Used with permission.

[7] Heidi Baker, Rolland Baker, *Expecting Miracles: True Stories of God's Supernatural Power and How You Can Experience It* (Grand Rapids, MI, Chosen Books, 2000).

[8] Firsthand account from Rolland Baker, April 2011. Used with permission.

Study Questions:

- What spoke to you most from this chapter?

- Share an experience you may have had with one of the spiritual gifts we just studied.

- What do you think is the key difference between cultivated faith and the *spiritual gift of faith?*

- What was your main takeaway regarding *gifts of healings?*

- Do you sense your faith arising, encouraging you to be more open to the Holy Spirit's marvelous gifts? Explain.

11
To Hear
His Voice

The Declarative Gifts

Declarative Gifts are our discussion topic for this chapter of study. These graces are the speaking gifts, the verbal declaring of God's heart or purposes. Indeed, the whole of Scripture is Holy Spirit inspired, revealing the nature and counsel of Almighty God **2 Timothy 3:16**. However, when these spiritual gifts are in use, they are particular messages given by the Lord for a specific moment in time to a particular person or group of people.

These spiritual graces must always agree and align with God's written Word, the Bible.

We have already discussed the private gift of prayer, known as speaking in tongues. Yet, Paul teaches there is also *a public gift of tongues* accompanied with *the gift of interpretation* in **1 Corinthians 12:10** and **1 Corinthians 14**. The following passages address the corporate use of these two gifts together, as they are only effective when displayed hand in hand.

Study each of the following verses, then state in your own words how the gift of tongues and the gift of interpretation were presented or taught. Also, add the resulting outcome of these gifts:

Acts 2:1-13

_____

_____

1 Corinthians 14:12-13

_____

_____

In your own words, write your definition of the *gift of tongues* working with the *gift of interpretation*. Why would these gifts be encouraging?

_____

_____

_____

Examples of the *gift of prophecy* are abundant in the New Testament. Please turn to the passages below. Relate how the people involved demonstrated this gift and what the results were.

Luke 1:67-79

_____

_____

Acts 21:8-14

_____

_____

1 Corinthians 14:3-4

_____

_____

Paul gives believers a strong admonition in **1 Thessalonians 5:19-21**. Please share how his words impact you.

_____

_____

_____

Please record your definition of the *gift of prophecy* and why this gift is beneficial and important for today:

_____

_____

_____

_____

—————————— ⑤ ——————

The Gifts of Tongues and Interpretation...

The *corporate or public gift of tongues* has the same benefits as the believer's private use of spiritual language: edification, worship, and revealing what is unknown. Nevertheless, the corporate use of this gift can sometimes be confusing. The fact that Paul wrote so much instruction for its use in the midst of a congregation leads me to believe that the Corinthian church was also a trifle stymied by the gift.

It appears that when the church in Corinth met together, many believers were praying out loud in their private prayer language. They were speaking out rather than waiting for the Holy Spirit to prompt them to express the separate and different gift of spiritual language with an attending interpretation. We may also experience the same difficulty in knowing *when* the Spirit would have us speak forth words of a spiritual language while in a group setting with interpretation.

Another possible reason that the *public gift of tongues* concerns us is that it requires a second element of interpretation for the gift to be valid. A person speaking out in a spiritual language in a meeting should first be convinced that either they personally will receive the interpretation of their message or that there are others present

The public gift of tongues requires interpretation.

who are familiar and somewhat practiced in the gift of interpretation. Oh my! How would a person know that? Therein is the difficulty.

However, we know that the Lord is not the author of confusion and that He is not trying to place this gift beyond our reach **1 Corinthians 14:1, 33**. Instead of *throwing the baby out with the bath water*, we may first have to become comfortable with these two gifts of the Spirit in a smaller group setting. We can accomplish this by our willingness to step out in faith while being sensitive to those present at a meeting, especially if there are believers who haven't yet experienced or had teaching about spiritual gifts. Paul calls these folks *uninformed* **1 Corinthians 14:23**.

It is usually best spiritual practice to first check with the leaders or pastors of any meeting before sharing spiritual gifts. What are the spiritual protocols for that segment of Christ's beloved body? We must always walk in His Spirit of gentleness with a willingness to yield to the consensus of those present. And, to the best of our ability, we should discern whether spiritual gifts are accepted and if the Lord is genuinely initiating what we are being prompted to do or say. Upon closer examination, Paul directs his rebuke to the Corinthians in **Chapter 14** at their *unwillingness* to yield or submit to each other so that all might be encouraged during their gatherings. Let's read again...

> *Do not **quench the Spirit**.*
> *Do not **despise prophecies**.*
> ***Test all things**, hold fast what is good.*
> **1 Thessalonians 5:19-21** (emphasis, mine)

As we read Paul's words, *we recognize his* admonition is not directed towards the gifts—instead, their improper use.

From what we notice in God's Word, the gifts of tongues and interpretation may be praise to God or prayer. These spiritual gifts may also be like a prophetic word, especially for an unbeliever's benefit.

In the law it is written:
"With men of other tongues and other lips I will speak to this
people; And yet, for all that, they will not hear Me," says the
Lord.

Therefore tongues are for a sign, not to those who believe but
to unbelievers; but prophesying is not for unbelievers but for
those who believe.
1 Corinthians 14:21-22 (Paul quoting Isaiah 28:11)

On the day of Pentecost, Jesus' disciples praised God's wonderful works in their new prayer languages. It is fitting that the gift of tongues and interpretation can be an act of worship as the Holy Spirit indwells Christians to glorify the Lord Jesus **John 4:23-24**. That day, the disciples were verbalizing in known earthly languages understood by those who did not yet believe in Christ.

Tongues can be
as sign to
the unbelieving.

These listeners later responded to the gospel due to the outpouring of this gift and Peter's preaching. This example indicates the truth of Paul's words above that the gift of tongues can be a sign to an unbeliever.

Although I have not yet personally witnessed an unbeliever coming to faith in Christ because someone spoke to them in their prayer language, I have heard and read numerous well-documented recent events where this miracle happened. These are thrilling stories where the Christians sensed the Holy Spirit prompting them to speak directly to an unbeliever in their spiritual language, or the incident occurred in a group setting where a gift of tongues was expressed in the person's known language.

Dr. Jack Hayford recounts a story from missionary Evelyn Thompson who served in the Philippines where she was called upon to minister to a woman who was under demonic influence.

> *I began to pray again, and as I did, out of my mouth—like a ball of fire from the middle of my stomach—came another language that I had never spoken before in the Spirit; certainly, a language that I had never learned, nor had I ever heard it before. But as it came...I saw a change in the expression on the face of the woman we were praying for. I saw that her eyes were listening, and at once I began to understand that I was speaking her language.*

> *...I saw the muscles in her face begin to relax, the trembling stopped, and her hands ceased the wild beating of the air as though she were trying to hit me...Then a most wonderful thing happened.*

> *I not only could see that she understood me, but suddenly I was enabled to understand what I was saying; I was able to think as well as to speak in a language which I had never heard before! In the following minutes I explained the story of Jesus Christ...And with perfect awareness, of every word I was speaking, I led her to the Lord Jesus Christ with full understanding of that language at that time.*

> *She was totally delivered and today she still lives. She became a witness to the resurrection power of the Lord Jesus Christ...I did not know that language after that one instance. I later heard that language spoken by others in the mountain areas but could not understand it and I certainly could not speak it.*[1]

The newly Spirit-baptized disciples in **Acts 2** spoke in known languages (although unknown to them) on that amazing morning. However, it is likely that many were also speaking in angelic or unknown tongues, which Paul writes about in **1 Corinthians 13:1**, as we have previously learned. I note this to illustrate that when a person feels prompted by the Spirit to speak out in a tongue, they shouldn't be concerned if their language is a known. The only requirement is that the message should have an interpretation. Paul instructs that if there isn't an interpretation following a tongue, the person speaking should keep silent **1 Corinthians 14:28.** I don't think he intended this as harshly as it might sound. It just means that the Corinthian Church was learning *how* to move in the gifts of the Spirit just as we are.

Several times, I thought I had the interpretation of a message given in a spiritual language. When this happened, words formed in my thoughts as the person spoke, or I had a *picture* in my mind. How the Holy Spirit might reveal an interpretation to a listener is solely up to Him. Once again, we must totally depend upon the Holy Spirit as we learn to hear His voice. When the person finished speaking, I then shared in English the praise, prayer, or message I sensed the Lord was saying. There have been times when I thought I had an interpretation of a message in tongues, but someone else began sharing ahead of me. In those situations, I've kept the following verse in mind:

> *But if anything is revealed to another who sits by, let the first keep silent.*
> **1 Corinthians 14:30**

If there seems to be more than one interpretation, as sometimes takes place, it may be that the tongue had also prompted a prophetic word. Regardless, if everyone takes their turn in sharing and is willing to yield, as Paul admonishes, every gift given can bring edification to a gathering of believers.

Several years ago, I was in a large prayer gathering, interceding fervently but quietly for my father, who had not yet responded positively to the Gospel. I remember weeping over the state of his heart. When I had exhausted how to pray for my dad in English, I began to intercede for him in my prayer language, under my breath. Unbeknownst to me, the person next to me had stopped praying and had started listening to me pray in the Spirit. She interrupted me to tell me that she understood my prayer language and that I was beseeching God to save my dad. She had no prior knowledge of the situation. Several years later, my elderly dad unexpectedly received Christ by faith!

Paul likens and gives equal footing to the gift of tongues with interpretation to the *gift of prophecy* **1 Corinthians 14:5**. He emphasizes that God can and does speak to His people through supernatural means to build faith and convince hearts **Isaiah 28:11, 1 Corinthians 14:21**.

Nothing is more inspiring than attending a meeting where the Holy Spirit moves and distributes gifts. Fortunately, from the onset of my Christian life, I have had excellent teaching regarding this subject. The few times I have been in situations where there was disorder or confusion, it was quickly diffused by instruction immediately provided by those in leadership. Rather than becoming scary incidents, the leaders turned the events into teaching times for everyone without embarrassing the parties involved. In turn, I have employed these lessons when facing moments needing further correction or explanation.

It is appropriate to pray in the Spirit when a group of believers gathers for prayer or praise and are informed about spiritual gifts. Recently, another sister in Christ and I met to intercede on behalf of a friend who had taken a serious turn from God, leaving her husband and children. We spent the day fasting—abstaining from food, or other practices, for spiritual purposes—on the woman's behalf **Isaiah 58:6-14**. We met later to pray together for our friend. That night, when we came to the end of all we knew to pray for our friend in English, we each began praying in the Spirit. The Lord supplied greater insight into how to pray more effectively in spiritual battle prayer to release our friend from the enemy's grip. We shortly saw our dear sister return to her faith in Christ with fresh surrender and her family restored.

During a prayer time for someone at a ministry event, I was prompted to speak out in tongues as I experienced an inner tugging at my heart and a sense of direction from the Holy Spirit. Before I gave the message, I told everyone what I was about to do and why. I then proceeded in a normal tone of voice but loud enough for everyone to hear. After the message, I shared what I believe was the interpretation—a prayer from God's heart for the person. Immediately following, others spoke prayers, pictures, and prophetic words. It was a special time of ministry for everyone, and it appeared helpful to give instruction beforehand, as I had learned previously from my spiritual mentors.

The Gift of Prophecy...

Paul encourages us to pursue love and to desire spiritual gifts at the outset of **1 Corinthians 14** but especially that we would prophesy. He reveals why he gives the *gift of prophecy* such high marks in **verse 3**. A prophetic word brings edification, exhortation, and comfort to those who hear it.

Paul encourages the gift of prophecy.

Let's look at the Greek word that our English Bible defines as *prophecy:*

Propheteia Greek—Meaning: From the words *pro*, forth, and *phemi*, to speak. *A discourse emanating from divine inspiration declaring God's purposes, whether by reproving or admonishing, bringing comfort, consolation, or encouragement.*

We must note that a prophetic word or any spiritual gift will never contradict the written canon of Scripture known as the Bible.

159

The Book of James confirms that God has no variation or shadow of turning **James 1:17**. He will not contradict His Word. The context of the whole of Scripture is the litmus test for a prophetic message. **Revelation 22:18** also records that we cannot and should not attempt to add to the Bible. A prophetic word is not a discourse of doctrine. Instead, it is a word of encouragement, comfort, guidance, foretelling of a future event, or an admonition shared in the immediacy of the circumstances and people for whom the word is given.

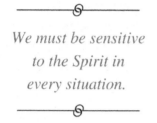

We must be sensitive to the Spirit in every situation.

It is also imperative that we are sensitive to the *way* a prophecy is delivered. We learned earlier that *the spirits of the prophets are subject to the prophets* **1 Corinthians 14:32**. Paul writes immediately following *that God is not the author of confusion but of peace* **verse 33**. We are also reminded in **James 3:16-17** that what the Lord initiates is *pure, peaceable, gentle, willing to yield, full of mercy and good fruits, without partiality, and with hypocrisy.* Even those words that might be difficult for a listener to hear can be given in a way to bring encouragement, demonstrating how the Lord speaks to His children.

We must also consider that a prophetic word may manifest itself through countless teachers, pastors, and evangelists. Their words may have been studied and prepared beforehand. Nonetheless, God will speak directly to individuals through their messages. How many times have we heard someone teach or share God's Word during a church service or event, and we have thought, *That person somehow knew exactly what I needed to hear!*

Dr. Jack Hayford writes this:

> *We have all frequently seen this kind of prophecy...It is usually manifested...thousands of times every week through pastors and teachers who deliver their messages and lessons*

with a distinct quality of the Holy Spirit's presence being sensed by those hearing them. This order of prophecy ought not be presumed or overlooked. It isn't prophecy because it's spoken, but because it's anointed. And it isn't better because it's presented by apparently better qualified people. God delights to speak through all his own; which leads to the second facet of prophecy—a functional manifestation of the Holy Spirit which may be realized by either a platformed or an unplatformed believer.[2]

An Individual Prophetic Word...

If you are sensing a prompting in your spirit that the Lord is giving you a prophetic word to share yet have a sense of agitation in your heart, be willing to yield and let the Holy Spirit calm you down. Our fleshly emotions can hinder what the Holy Spirit is trying to accomplish, thereby muddying the waters. I remember a woman in our church who occasionally delivered prophetic words with an intensity that bordered on condemnation. The words themselves were not harsh, but they were spoken with abrasiveness causing the congregation to feel vulnerable. Randy met privately with the woman and her husband, providing gentle correction, and pulling from the prophetic messages those genuinely timely portions. We all learned a good lesson, and the woman was not unduly embarrassed.

That the Holy Spirit would use imperfect human vessels to impart His word is beyond me. He is much more trusting than I am! With that said, there may be times when we or someone else may *not* get it right. Grace is needed for each other as we grow in experiencing the gifts of the Holy Spirit. However, if someone speaks a supposed prophetic word, put the message to the test with these questions:

- Does the message parallel the written Word of God—is it scripturally sound?
- Does the word confirm something you already sense or know?

- What is the tone of the message?
- What is the character of the person giving the word?
- Does the prophecy bring peace, hope, or understanding, or is it causing confusion, dread, or hurt?

If someone gives you a personal prophetic word, ask the Lord if it truly is from Him. The Spirit will bring a sense of resonance with the *rightness* of the message to your heart and mind.

Prophecy usually confirms something that Lord Jesus has already been telling you. It is wise to share a word of prophecy someone gives you with others you trust or *table* the message until it is proven or disproven. If it is from God, it will happen. Doing this is my consistent practice. This week, a longtime family friend contacted Randy concerning a prophetic word someone gave him, wisely requesting a *second opinion* before responding to what he had been told **Proverbs 11:14**.

> *Prophecy usually confirms something you already know.*

Once, a church staff member of ours was given a supposed prophetic word from a person with a respected prophetic ministry in the United States that she would be married within the year. However, when she shared this message with the rest of the church staff, not one of us believed it was from the Lord. This message almost shipwrecked the woman's life several months later when she met someone that was not a godly man. She seriously considered marrying him, feeling pressured by the prophetic message. Thankfully, she broke off the relationship.

Because of the human element when dispensing any of the spiritual gifts, it is wise to preface any prophetic message with a disclaimer. Consider saying, *I sense the Lord might be saying,* or *I believe that the Holy Spirit wants to tell us, or I am not sure if this is God, but...* then give the message. We must be aware that our emotions can distort what the Holy Spirit is doing or saying. We may want God to do something because we feel so deeply for a person that we confuse our emotions with His prompting. We must discern what we are thinking and feeling before ministering.

I am very reticent to say, *God is saying, the Lord wants you to know,* or be so emphatic that a message doesn't leave room for human error. Many may disagree that it is not wise to give a disclaimer because it nullifies the prophetic word. However, I believe that the person on the receiving end of the gift will recognize if the message is truly from the Lord Jesus by how it impacts their heart and life. If it is from God, they will know it.

Once again, let's read these two passages together:

> *How is it then, brethren? Whenever you come together, each of you has a psalm, has a teaching, has a tongue, has a revelation, has an interpretation. Let all things be done for edification.*
> **1 Corinthians 14:26**

> *But the manifestation of the Spirit is given to each one for the profit of all...*
> **1 Corinthians 12:7**

Evangelist Reinhard Bonnke writes:

> *The expression "the profit of all" in 1 Corinthians 12:7 is the Greek word **Sympheron**, from which comes the English word "symphony." The Holy Spirit is a Composer conducting His own work, bringing counterpoint and harmony from many interlocking themes and instruments. He doesn't need or want everyone playing the same tune. "There are diversities of gifts, but the same Spirit. There are differences of ministries, but the same Lord. And there are diversities of activities, but it is the same God who works all in all."*
> *1Corinthians 12:4-6.[3]*

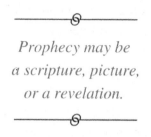

Prophecy may be a scripture, picture, or a revelation.

A prophetic utterance may be a scripture, a picture, or a revelation given to someone. When Bible verses are given as a prophetic word, the Lord is communicating a *rhema-now* word that Jesus refers to in **Luke 4:4** or when Paul references it as a weapon in spiritual warfare prayer **Ephesians 6:17**.[4] The message may begin as a single word or phrase that the Holy Spirit then provides a broader perspective. Sometimes, a person may sense what they are to say well before the time of its delivery. On other occasions, similar to what a few of the Old and New Testament prophets experienced, the Holy Spirit may prompt a person to perform an action that will physically display what God is communicating **Ezekiel 4, Hosea 1, Acts 21:10-11**.

Let's look at some modern-day examples of the gift of prophecy.

Randy and I always end our week-long teaching times for the mission organization Youth With a Mission (YWAM) in Taipei, Taiwan, with a time of praying for each student and staff member. Countless times, the Holy Spirit has provided us with prophetic words, or words of knowledge or wisdom that have later proven to be from Him. All glory to Jesus and not our often-feeble spirituality!

One notable instance was a young man I was praying for, where I sensed the Lord giving me a picture of him cutting a path through a dense jungle with a machete. It seemed the Lord was telling the young missionary to have confidence in what He would be working through his life and calling. A few years later, many staff members who remembered the prophetic word related that the young man had just taken an assignment in South America, in the heart of the Amazon jungle, translating the Bible into a dialect of the region. He was literally carving a path for God's Word to touch an unreached people group.

While we were in a group prayer time regarding the launch of a new pioneer church, a woman related *a picture* she saw in her mind. She *envisioned* various puzzle pieces suspended in the air. One by one, the Lord gently placed them on a table below. Immediately, another person praying with us gave the interpretation of the picture. Jesus was saying that we were not to force the puzzle pieces of our new move into their positions or push hard on them to make them fit as we planted the new church. Neither were we to try to make the puzzle pieces move faster. In other words, the Lord had perfect timing and positioning in getting the church started, and we were not to get in the way!

Randy and I were sitting in a church service with hundreds of believers when he sensed the Holy Spirit nudging him to give a prophetic word to an individual in attendance. Randy had no clue who the person might be and only had the first few words of what he was to say. As Randy struggled with what to do, a pause came in the meeting, and Randy approached the pastor for permission to share. The pastor, who knew Randy well, agreed.

In front of the congregation, Randy shared there was a woman present who wanted to give God one last chance to speak to her before filing for divorce from her husband and leaving her faith altogether (a word of knowledge). Next, Randy prophesied that if the woman would only wait a few days longer, God would do a mighty miracle in saving her husband and gloriously restoring her marriage.

Immediately after the service, a woman we didn't know who was sitting directly behind us tugged at Randy's sleeve to say that she was the person to whom the Lord was speaking. With mascara streaming, she explained that her husband had locked her and their children out of their home just the night before in a fit of rage. The woman had come to the church service telling God she was *throwing in the towel* regarding her faith and marriage. Yet through Randy's message, she heard the Lord telling her to hang on just a little bit longer.

About a month later, the pastor of the church excitedly contacted Randy. The woman had returned home after that Sunday service where she discovered her husband was remorseful and repentant. He then came to see a pastor in the church that same week and surrendered his life to Christ. He was immediately baptized in water the following weekend, and as a couple, they were beginning marital counseling.

During a difficult season of transition—I spoke of this in an earlier chapter—Randy and I were in a quandary mid-move of owning one home and moving to a rental. Our original home was headed for foreclosure as our renters unexpectedly bailed out of their rental contract with us. At a church service, a man we barely knew felt led to pray for us. He had no clue about our circumstances but sensed the Holy Spirit prompting him to tell us that our future was *not foreclosure but profit*. In essence, this was a word of knowledge with prophetic encouragement.

Our home actually went into foreclosure. Nevertheless, a last-minute buyer contacted the mortgage company with a viable offer which was accepted! I am not a financial prosperity proponent—believing it is the prosperity of the soul and spirit that Jesus speaks of in **John 10:10**—however, from that moment forward, our finances began to fall into place, and they have remained solid through two recessions to this day.

The Holy Spirit may use physical items or gestures to speak to us, as we read in **Acts 21:10-11**.

The Lord separately prompted Randy and me to begin a teaching series on spiritual warfare for our congregation's men and women. The teaching times coincided perfectly with various issues arising in our lives and those in our flock.

A few weeks into the teaching, my former workplace—a county fire department from which I had retired—presented me with a real-deal, beautifully mounted fire axe. The axe had been misplaced and stored for four years at the fire department headquarters before being found and given to me. I was unable to tell Randy about my gift until the next day when he came home from a men's conference where our Men's Institute group had won an exquisite, authentic sword for having a high percentage of men from the church in attendance.

Randy and I admired each other's weaponry, had a good chuckle about carrying our heavy arsenal around, and didn't give the axe and sword another thought. Yet, a few days I sensed the Holy Spirit speaking to me. The Lord was reminding us through these weapons of our authority in Christ, and He did not want us to take lightly the spiritual warfare that we currently found ourselves in because He didn't! I cannot express how encouraging this prophetic, physical picture became during that season in our lives.

The *positives* of an authentic gift of prophecy far outweigh any negative aspects of the misuse of the gift. Paul admonishes the Thessalonian Church that they should not despise prophesying, and neither should we **1 Thessalonians 5:20**. Timely, Holy Spirit-led prophetic words are like *apples of gold in settings of silver* **Proverbs 25:11**. These words can turn the tide of a believer's heart from doubt to faith, discouragement to victory, and uncertainty into hope or direction.

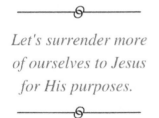

Let's surrender more of ourselves to Jesus for His purposes.

As we close this chapter on the *Declarative Gifts,* let's take a moment and ask the Lord to help us surrender to Him in more significant measure for His purposes. Let's request His aid in strengthening us to become more available to encourage, exhort, admonish in love, and comfort others. Asking Jesus, the One and Only, that His love always be the first and highest pursuit of our lives, and the power and blessing of spiritual gifts may increase in us to His glory alone. Amen.

---

[1] Jack Hayford, *The Beauty of Spiritual Language: My Journey Toward the Heart of God* (Dallas, TX; Word Publishing, 1992), page 121.

[2] Ibid, pages 84-85.

[3] Reinhard Bonnke, *Holy Spirit: Are We Flammable or Fireproof* (Orlando, FL; Christ for all Nations, 2017), pages 146-147.

[4] *Rhema* is the Greek word for *word* translated in these passages Luke 4:4, Ephesians 6:17. Differing from the Greek *logos* (also translated as *word*) that means a discourse or the whole of the Bible, a *rhema* is that section of God's Word that provides what is needed in an immediate or now situation.

Study Questions:

- What spoke to you most from this chapter?

- Share an experience you may have had with one of the spiritual gifts we just studied.

- Has the Holy Spirit had the opportunity to work either His *gift of interpretation of tongues* or *prophecy* through you? How did you sense His prompting (for example, a picture, phrase, scripture…)?

- From the bullet list of questions on *pages 161-162* that ask what you should consider when someone appears to be giving a prophetic word, which question do you think is the most important and why?

- How were you encouraged that the Holy Spirit works through the church like a composer of a symphony?

12
Sustaining
His Overflow

If someone were to inquire what I thought were the most essential elements in a believer's life for living in the Holy Spirit's overflow, I would name these three aspects:

- To be aware of and available for all the Holy Spirit provides.
- To have experiential knowledge of God's Word.
- To walk in ever-increasing intimacy with God.

We have spent our entire study—still only scratching the surface—of Who the Holy Spirit is, His work, and spiritual gifts. Now, we will conclude our time together with the other two distinctives of Spirit-filled living.

As with anything pertaining to God, there are no formulas. We aren't called to religion but to an intimate relationship. We are not called to legalism that supports spiritual pride on the one hand and dismal shame on the other. Yet we find throughout God's Word that a dynamic and personal knowledge of God's Word and entering the Lord's presence through times alone with Him are the hallmarks of the men and women we admire most in the Bible and throughout the church age since Jesus' resurrection.

Turn to **John 1:14**. Ponder this verse. If Jesus is the *Living Word of God,* how might that impact our reading the written Word of God, the Bible?

_____

_____

_____

_____

Psalm 119 is dedicated to glorifying and revealing the power of God's Word. Let's take a look at just a few of its verses. What do you discover? Note that synonyms for *word* might be testimonies, law, commandments, or precepts depending on your Bible translation.

Verse 11

_____

Verse 24

_____

Verse 105

_____

Verse 127

_____

Psalm 107:20 could have a variety of meanings, and every one of them would probably be correct! Read it now and share how it might apply to your life currently.

_____

_____

Look at **Luke 4:4** where Jesus is quotes **Deuteronomy 8:3**. What does He compare God's word with? _____

How important is the comparison item to your own life?

_____

Think of Jesus saying that bread represents a broader comparison to the food we eat to sustain our lives. Have you ever missed more than two or three meals? How did you feel, or what happened to you?

_____

_____

Why do you think Jesus makes such a strong comparison between life-nourishing bread and God's Word? Consider **Job 23:12** when you write your response.

_____

_____

_____

Let's look at **Hebrews 4:12-13**. Share your thoughts about why the Bible is like no other book written.

_____

_____

_____

Let's now examine the simple yet profound experience of walking in intimacy with God. Turn to King David's heart cry found in **Psalm 27:4**. How does this verse minister to your heart?

_____

_____

King David shares more concerning an intimate walk with God. Look at **Psalm 16:11** and share the promises you find here.

_____

_____

We have all gleaned much regarding the story of Mary and Martha found in **Luke 10:38-42**. What is the one thing Lord Jesus refers to in **verse 42** and its implications for your life?

_____

_____

_____

Matthew 6:6 in the New King James Version of the Bible calls time alone with God as being with Him in the *secret place*. What does the phrase *secret place* mean to you in the context of drawing near to the Lord?

_____

_____

As always, we take our cues from Jesus for living life in the *dynamis* of the Holy Spirit. We have already looked at some of the many examples about His taking time to be alone with the Father in **Matthew 14:23, Mark 6:46**, and **Luke 5:16**. Open to **John 5:19**. How does this speak to your heart regarding time alone with God and being led by the Holy Spirit, just as Jesus was led by the Father?

_____

_____

_____

Finally, turn to **Revelation 3:20**. What does it mean for you to dine with Jesus?

_____

_____

⎯⎯⎯⎯⎯⎯ ☙ ⎯⎯⎯⎯⎯⎯

Holy Spirit Power Through His Word...

The written Word will always lead us to and reveal the Living Word, Jesus **John 1:14,** just as the Holy Spirit does **John 16:13-14.**

The Bible truly reveals Jesus to us, draws us closer to Him, and speaks into our lives daily to ascertain what the Holy Spirit is speaking to us. And through our study of the Holy Spirit, we find that it is imperative that we know what His Word says so that we can walk in godly discernment of what is taking place around us at any given moment.

We learn something amazing about the Bible from Paul in his letter to his protégé, Timothy:

> *All scripture is **God-breathed** and is useful for teaching, rebuking, correcting and training in righteousness, so that the servant of God may be thoroughly equipped for every good work.*
> **2 Timothy 3:16-17** NIV (emphasis, mine)

Knowing the Bible is a living and *God-breathed* book changes everything about how we view it. We have learned that the Holy Spirit *is* God's breath, and we can conclude that He is the author of this Marvelous Book. Just as our bodies can't live without oxygen, our souls and spirits need God's life breath daily. It will revitalize us when we feel weak, remind us of His promises, speak directly into our current situations, and lead us into His truth.

All of scripture is God-breathed...

God's life breath through His Word ushers in His felt presence in the Holy Spirit. If we read the Bible without the Spirit's help, it is merely words on a page. On the other hand, without the anchor of His Word, the power and presence of the Holy Spirit can leave us open to trusting only in what we feel, leading to emotional responses that won't stand in life's storms or may even lead us astray.

Together, God's Word *and* the Holy Spirit who wrote it are an explosive, powerful, healing, saving, and delivering combination bringing the rule of heaven to earth.

> *But Jesus answered him, saying, "It is written, 'Man shall not live by bread alone, but by every word of God.'*
> **Luke 4:4**

Along with being our spiritual oxygen, the Bible is also our *daily bread*. If we neglect it, our spirits can become anemic because His living Word is spiritual food for our lives **Hebrews 5:12-14**. It cuts through all the stuff of our soul and gets to the matters of the Spirit, which in turn, brings healing to our soul—the arena of our thoughts, emotions, personality, intellect, and ability to choose.

When we are spiritually depleted, it is like going to the market while our stomachs are hungry. We load up our shopping carts with junk food that generally wouldn't tempt us. Our life in God's Word is like that, too. When our souls and spirits are filled and saturated with a delicious feast and fresh Holy Spirit oxygen from the Bible, we are less likely to indulge in temptations and distractions. These hindrances will ultimately not satisfy us. However, when we daily hear God's voice speaking to us through His Word or sense that He is saying something directly to us that His written Word confirms, we become more in tune with what the Holy Spirit is working around us.

Logos and Rhema...

As we continually walk in the daily overflow of the Holy Spirit, His Word is indispensable for His hearing His voice correctly and sensing His leading.

There are two keywords from the original New Testament Greek that are used in the Scriptures to reveal how God works through His written Word to speak to us. From **John 1:14**, which we read earlier regarding Jesus being the Word of God, we find the Greek word used here—*logos*.

Logos Greek—Meaning: *the transmission of something being said, a thought, a communication, a discourse, or a speech. Logos* is the word used for *divine declarations, precepts, instruction, doctrine, and promises.*

The Lord Jesus is the *Living Logos*. The word also describes the Bible as the whole of God's counsel to humanity. As we make a daily habit of coming to the banquet of *God's Logos* and inviting the Holy Spirit to reveal Jesus to us, we are steadily being transformed and growing in more significant Holy Spirit awareness in our lives. **John 14:21**.

There is also another Greek word used in the New Testament for *word*...

> *And take the helmet of salvation, and the sword of the*
> *Spirit, which is the* **word** *of God;*
> **Ephesians 6:17** (Emphasis, mine)

A *rhema* word is one of the pieces of God's Armor found in *Ephesians 6:10-18*. This type of *word*, differing from *logos*, is our offensive weapon–*our sword in the Holy Spirit*–used to encourage us and defeat the devil in any circumstance that would overwhelm us.

Rhema Greek—Meaning: *to speak, a statement, or a word uttered by a living voice.*

The *New Spirit-Filled Life Bible* states it this way...

> *In reference to the Bible,* **logos** *is the Bible in its entirety;*
> **rhema** *is a verse from the Bible. The meaning of rhema in distinction to logos is illustrated in* **Ephesians 6:17**,
> *where the reference is not to the Scriptures as a whole,*

*but to that portion which the believer wields as a sword in
time of need.*[1]

A *rhema* word from God is a *now* word for a current or coming situation.
It is a divine encouragement and most definitely can be a prophetic word.
It can also be a weapon from God in our mouths in times of spiritual
warfare or our need for Holy Spirit discernment.

When Jesus quoted from **Deuteronomy 8:3,** *It is written, 'Man shall not
live by bread alone, but by every **word** that proceeds from the mouth of
God.'* The Greek word He spoke here was *rhema.* Here, Jesus shows us
how to employ a Spirit-directed Bible passage to declare God's dominion,
truth, and power when we face any difficult situation, especially our
enemy.

Now, we can see why the Holy Spirit working
in tandem with His Word can be so effective
in our lives and in our ministry for others.
Knowing God's Word for ourselves and
reading it expectantly to hear His voice can
change everything for us.

*The Holy Spirit
works in tandem
with His Word.*

It is a very subjective matter in discerning when God gives you a direct
Scripture—a *rhema* word—for your given circumstance or need. Indeed,
anyone can pull out a verse from the Bible and make it say what they want.
There is a danger in doing that, and certainly, that has led to an abuse of
God's Word for misguided purposes. Nevertheless, the rewards of
someone sensing that the Holy Spirit is giving them a specific word for a
situation is greater than the few people who would attempt to twist His
Word to their own desires.

Hearing the Holy Spirit speaking directly to your spirit from the Bible,
encouraging your soul, providing guidance and next steps, and as an
anchor to stand upon in faith in a time of trial is one of the most thrilling
aspects of overflowing life in the Holy Spirit.

A Daily Feast...

Let's read the Bible both devotionally and as students.

When reading to hear what the Holy Spirit might be speaking to us daily, let's invite Him to direct where He desires to take us. Ask yourself...

- What is He saying?
- Is there a particular book or chapter He wants me to open?
- Is there a particular passage that He wants me to linger in?
- Does He lead me to cross-reference (found in many Bible margins) another verse that will amplify His Word to me?
- What do my Bible study notes have to offer?

I read God's Word devotionally, for study, and for *distance*. Meaning, I read a large portion of scripture at a time, mining the wealth of the original Bible languages. Reading larger segments of the Scriptures also helps me to grasp what was taking place at the time of its writing. I will also read commentaries or Bible studies from men and women whose love for God and His Word evidenced a greater measure of the Holy Spirit, which has significantly benefited my life.

For years, I felt tremendous guilt (I cannot over-emphasize this) when I missed a day or two, or weeks on end, falling *off the wagon* of reading God's Word. This was especially true when attempting to read through the Bible in a year by working through a prescribed Bible reading plan. Recently, I have been able to do this, although seldom finishing on time—but with no condemnation!

Honestly, guilt is never a motivator for doing anything from the heart, and it certainly isn't from Jesus. Guilt will also quench the Holy Spirit faster than you can blink! Confidently ask the Lord for a fresh hunger and take the first steps of opening up the Bible in an easy-to-read translation, receiving just the word you need today. The Lord will not disappoint.

Intimacy with God...

King David from the Old Testament and Mary from the New Testament share with us their secret for living the abundant life Jesus promises to His followers. Time alone with Him, cultivating His felt presence in the Holy Spirit, and hearing His voice—what the New King James Version of the Bible calls the *secret place* in many passages **Psalm 27:5, 31:20, Matthew 6:18.**[2]

> *He who dwells in the **secret place** of the Most High*
> *Shall abide under the shadow of the Almighty.*
> **Psalm 91:1**

> *But you, when you pray, go into your room, and when you have shut your door, pray to your Father who is in the **secret place**; and your Father who sees in secret will reward you openly.*
> **Matt 6:6**

I like to think these verses call this time alone with God as the *secret place* because it is a place only you and He can come to alone, together. He has words meant only for you to hear from His heart **Psalm 25:14**. He wants to satisfy and refresh you, providing a bountiful meal for your soul **Psalm 23:5**.

> *Behold, I stand at the door and knock. If anyone hears My voice and opens the door, I will come in to him and dine with him, and he with Me.*
> **Revelation 3:20**

> *You prepare a table before me in the presence of my enemies;*
> *You anoint my head with oil;*
> *My cup runs over.*
> **Psalm 23:5**

Why are these quiet times alone with the Lord so necessary to living in the overflow of the Holy Spirit? It is because they are where we encounter God Himself, filling, flooding, and healing our souls—and even our bodies. And from that place of personal fullness, we then discover the bounty of giving ourselves to ministry where we will seldom, if ever, experience burn-out because of Holy Spirit fullness and overflow. Because we are leaning into the Spirit's leading and not what we think we should be doing or giving away. It is here we discover the power of God and hear His voice giving us needed strength, encouragement, and direction directly from the Holy Spirit.

From personal experience and seeing hundreds of people find continuing transformation, healing, and empowerment for ministry in God's presence, it indeed is the *one thing* that Jesus spoke of that must become our priority. Most certainly, we count as heroes of the Bible and the current

The 'One Thing' time alone with Lord Jesus.

church age, those men and women who cultivated encountering the presence of the Holy Spirit in their times alone with the Father and the Son.

Living in a broken and fallen world, we *will* have times of trial, testing, tragedy, and persecution. Nevertheless, God's Word consistently promises streams in the desert and rivers in the wilderness **Isaiah 35:6-7, 43:19-21, Ephesians 3:16-20.**

This quiet time with Jesus is not where we come to Him and bring our laundry list of prayer requests. No, the Lord is calling us to come be with Him for a while, to be refreshed by His presence. He longs to spend time alone with you, and it is our highest privilege to respond to Him. What Adam and Eve lost with God, we can regain.[3]

Practical Tips...

Just as you would protect a young seedling from the elements that would destroy it, we need to learn how to cultivate and nurture a quiet time alone with God without distraction. Here are some practical tips:

- **Put on your calendar scheduled times alone with God like you would your best friend.** Give yourself a good half-hour or more. Without adding to your plate of to-dos, this is not your everyday time with Jesus; this is a separate time to worship and wait upon Him and hear what the Holy Spirit has to say. Not the other way around.
- **The best time to meet with Jesus is when you are at your best.** Pastor Wayne Cordeiro shares this encouragement in his book, *Divine Mentor*.[4] When are you most awake? Morning, afternoon, or evening? Make that your time to schedule being with the Lord.

- **Arrange for someone to watch the kids, dogs, duties, or whatever requires your oversight so that you will have uninterrupted time.**

- **Put your phone in another room and remove every distraction possible.** Bring a notebook if it helps to jot down some stray but important reminders that come to your thoughts, so you don't start obsessing about what you might forget. Crazy, but true. Don't be discouraged if training your thoughts to stay on Jesus takes practice! We all get distracted, but His Holy Spirit will help us. We just need to come.

- **Get comfortable.** Bring your Bible and a journal to record what you think He is saying to you from His Word and His heart **Jeremiah 30:2**. Come expecting a *rhema* word or He might reemphasize a word He has already given you. It is during these times that the Holy Spirit may reveal things in your life that are hindering you and He desires to break their grip. He will share His truth to replace these old patterns of thinking and feeling. You will often want to go back and remind yourself of what He has spoken to you.

- **Keep it simple.** Ask Jesus to join you. Truthfully, He has been waiting for you! There is no magic formula; if there were, your time alone with the Lord would become just another to-do list from religiosity. Instead, you are waiting for the Holy Spirit's leading **Romans 8:14**.

- **Worship.** Worship focuses our heart and mind on the Lord and attunes us to His presence **Psalm 22:3**. Pastor Randy Remington states: *worship interrupts our preoccupation with ourselves.*[5] The psalms are great for worship inspiration. Try softly—or loudly—singing your favorite praise and worship songs or worship in your spiritual language. Yes, this is a wonderful time for praying and singing in tongues! For some, playing worship music is helpful, but don't let it become distracting if you use your phone.

- **Let the Holy Spirit lead you.** We not only cultivate experiencing the Lord's presence, but we are also growing in letting the Spirit lead us, too. We are learning to be continually filled to overflowing with Him in our lives. Take baby steps. If a thought comes to mind—a picture or a Bible verse—what do you think the Lord is saying to you? [6] One thing might lead to something else, or one Bible verse might reference another until you land where Jesus is leading you. You will seldom lack knowing God's will for your life when you make these quiet times your priority **Romans 12:1-2**.

- **Don't get discouraged your first time.** Like priming the pump on a deep well that we haven't drawn water from for a long time, it may take a few meetups before the dust is knocked off our spirit. Remember, the Lord desires this time with you more than you do!

- **This time will be challenged.** The enemy of your soul knows the value and power of God's experienced presence. Everything under the sun might happen out of the blue as you attempt to make your date with the Lord. And yes, there will be times you may need to reschedule with Jesus, however, do so right away. The adversary knows that wherever Jesus is, people are set free. Press through when this time is challenged, or if you must, reschedule as soon as possible.

As you persist in prioritizing the *secret place*, you will find genuine refreshment, restoration, and rivers of living water in the Holy Spirit. You will find yourself growing in greater confidence in His leading, and your faith will be built upon the foundation of His Word ignited by His life breath. You will also

Let's live in Holy Spirit overflow!

not want to go back to living life without this precious and powerful time with God. He created you for this with Him, and you will receive what you need from Him directly. When the storms of unexpected circumstances, tragedy, or peril occur, your time alone with Jesus and His Word is your rock to stand on. And the Holy Spirit, the great Comforter and Counselor, will direct your steps.

> *They are abundantly satisfied with the fullness of Your house, And You give them drink from the river of Your pleasures.*
> **Psalms 36:8**

---

[1] Jack W. Hayford, Litt.D, Executive Editor, *New Spirit-Filled Life Bible, Third Edition* (Thomas Nelson, Nashville TN, 2018) Word Wealth at Matthew 4:4.

[2] Psalm 27:5, Psalm 31:20, Matthew 6:18

[3] Sue Boldt, *CrossPointe #1 – Building a Firm Foundation* (Charleston, SC: Kindle Direct Publishing), 2011, page 56.

[4] Wayne Cordeiro, The Divine Mentor (Grand Rapids, MI: Bethany House Publishers, 2007), page 109.

[5] Randy Remington, President: International Church of the Foursquare Gospel, *Converge Event*, Santa Clarita, CA – September 23-24, 2019.

[6] 1 Corinthians 14:26. This verse describes the many ways the Lord may speak to us.

Study Questions:

- What spoke to you most from this chapter?

- Share what God's Word means to you?

- Have you ever received a *rhema* scripture from the Lord? Recall it here:

- Record the things that might hinder or distract you most from taking time in the *secret place* with Lord Jesus.

- Share your thoughts about living life in the abundance of the Holy Spirit no matter what your current circumstances might be.

It's Only
the Beginning...

It happened just yesterday.

I was in one of those department stores with designer names at low prices with my cherished grandson, looking for a special toy to purchase. A woman approached me somewhere between looking at the big red fire truck and the bright yellow cement mixer toys. This unknown person requested my opinion on which pretty comforter she should buy to take to her hospital for an upcoming surgery. We discussed the various colors of the bedding she was considering. We both agreed on the flowery blanket— the stripey one was a bit too severe! Without a moment's hesitation, I then asked the stranger if I could pray for her.

I have stated that the Holy Spirit doesn't just grab you by the collar and make you do something, but honestly, this was the most natural thing in the world to do, and the words came out of my mouth instantly. The woman exclaimed that she would love for me to pray for her, and she promptly told me what the surgery concerned (her back). We held hands in the middle of the store, and I prayed for her healing.

I had no clue, going into the prayer, if she was a Christian. However, it was soon evident that she was a believer in her words of agreement with mine. When the prayer was over, we knew it was a divine appointment.

No, I do not know the outcome of her story. Nevertheless, I know God was at work in the middle of an ordinary day in both of our lives, encouraging us with His goodness.

Pastor Mark Batterson writes:

> *The Celtic Christians had a fascinating name for the Holy Spirit. They called Him An-Geadh-Glas, which means "wild goose." Can you think of a better description of what it's like to like to live a Spirit-led life than "wild goose chase"? When you follow the leading of the Holy Spirit, you never know who you'll meet, where you'll go, or what you'll do. But one thing is certain: it'll be anything but boring!*[1]

That is life in the Spirit. That is the life I want to live daily with all of my heart. And I know you do, too.

I pray this study has encouraged, challenged, enlightened, and made you thirsty for more of the Holy Spirit's breath in and upon your life. Reading our study passages from God's Word and remembering only a few out of multitudes of past experiences has increased my hunger for more of Him. I pray that a *supernatural* way of life will become our *natural* way of living. Let's see His wind continually removing anything from our lives that keep us from experiencing more of His presence, bringing the fire of revival that only He can ignite.

Indeed, Jesus' resurrection is our beginning, just as we read in the opening verse of the Book of Acts.

> *The former account I made, O Theophilus, of all that Jesus **began** both to do and teach...*
> **Acts 1:1** (emphasis added)

Let's continue being filled to overflowing—saturated, immersed, doused, and set ablaze with the Spirit of the Living God. For the sake of a dying, weary world that needs to see His power and love on display; for His glory alone. Doesn't living a *pneuma life* sound good?

Holy Spirit, come!

On the last day, that great day of the feast, Jesus stood and cried out, saying, "If anyone thirsts, let him come to Me and drink.

He who believes in Me, as the Scripture has said, out of his heart will flow rivers of living water."

But this He spoke concerning the Spirit, whom those believing in Him would receive; for the Holy Spirit was not yet given, because Jesus was not yet glorified.
John 7:37-39

The Spirit of the Lord GOD is upon Me,
Because the LORD has anointed Me
To preach good tidings to the poor;
He has sent Me to heal the brokenhearted,
To proclaim liberty to the captives,
And the opening of the prison to those who are bound.
Isaiah 61:1

Be glad then, you children of Zion,
And rejoice in the LORD your God;

For He has given you the former rain faithfully,
And He will cause the rain to come down for you—

The former rain,

And the latter rain in the first month.
The threshing floors shall be full of wheat,
And the vats shall overflow with new wine and oil...
I will pour out My Spirit on all flesh...
Joel 2:23-28

...Not by might
Nor by power,
But by My Spirit,'
Says the Lord of Hosts.
Zechariah 4:6

...You shall receive the gift of the Holy Spirit.
For the promise is to you and to your children,
And to all who are afar off,
As many as the Lord our God will call.
Acts 2:39

---

[1] Mark Batterson, **Draw the Circle: The 40 Day Prayer Challenge** (Grand Rapids, MI: Zondervan, 2012), page 18.

Hearing
From Others

Please enjoy reading the stories of men and women of various ages and backgrounds. Each of them was eager to share their experiences in the Holy Spirit with you! I cannot thank them enough for taking the time out of their busy schedules to write their initial encounter with the Holy Spirit's baptism.

These personal accounts will cause you to smile and rejoice. I hope you will be able to relate to at least one or more of them. The Lord is faithful to every life that seeks Him.

And you will seek Me and find Me,
When you search for Me with all your heart.
I will be found by you, says the Lord...
Jeremiah 29:13,14a

Be blessed as you read!

Kareen...

When I was fourteen, my friends brought me to a *Baptist Youth* event. There was an altar call, and my friend gave me *the look*, so I answered that call. I was not exactly sure what I was really doing then.

It wasn't until two years later that I began to seek the Lord and went to a *Catholic Teen Weekend*. After the retreat, I attended follow-up meetings on Friday nights to learn more about God. These events were led by my friend's father, *Brother Benny*. At the weekend retreat, Brother Benny spoke in tongues. I later heard him pray in his spiritual language in subsequent Friday night youth meetings. On Friday nights, hearing him pray in this unknown language was usually my cue with my friends to walk outside because we felt uncomfortable. Not once did Brother Benny explain to us what was happening to him. We thought that he was just a little crazy!

Later, I attended a different non-Catholic youth group. It was then that I truly accepted the Lord in my life and may have experienced Spirit baptism. I say this because I had an unexplainable encounter at a summer camp. I was sitting alone at night, crying out to God-recommitting my life to Him. I felt so cleansed. Afterward, I began to desire to know the Lord and obey Him.

I knew I needed to grow in my faith. For ten years, I fellowshipped in a new church that discipled me about God and His Word; however, the pastors never mentioned Holy Spirit baptism. Ever. They taught me the incredible disciplines of walking with the Lord by reading His Word and obeying Him, but I was not encouraged to walk in the power of the Holy Spirit or pursue His gifts. In fact, the church leadership believed that speaking in tongues was not something a church should be doing today.

In my hunger for more of God, a close friend introduced me to *Crossroads Church*. When you and Randy became its pastors, your introduction to the Holy Spirit's working was initially very uncomfortable for me. But the Lord used you both to present it to the congregation in such a gentle and confirming way. Because I developed such respect for you both, I thought to myself, *if you guys are teaching this to us, it can't be as bad as what I was taught many years ago!* However, I was still very hesitant and fearful of learning about tongues.

I hid the fear well because deep down inside, I truly wanted to experience more of the Lord. So, in your graceful way, you encouraged me to dig deeper. With your many examples, I could shed those fears and negative opinions about having a spiritual language.

I remember sitting on my bed, asking the Lord to fill me, waiting upon Him. I began to feel a surge within me, almost like my breath was getting taken away by a large gust of wind that somehow pushed through my insides and whirled in and out of me. *I thought to myself–is this it? Is this the experience that Sue was talking about?*

I began to try to speak but still had a little doubt mixed with fear. A few syllables started to come out: *fafafa...lalalala*, and then, of course, I began to think of the Christmas song, *Deck the Halls!* I felt like I was just experimenting instead of experiencing, so it took a while before I could completely relax and *surrender* my voice to the Holy Spirit. Months, in fact. But as I surrendered, He began to speak fluently through me, giving me the ability to start and stop.

As others around me began to experience the Holy Spirit and His gifts, too, I was encouraged even more. Now, it is a gift that I feel very privileged to have. I am excited to have this special language with my Lord.

Pneuma Life has opened a whole new world for me. An exciting, beautiful, abundant world for me that I never thought could be possible on this side of heaven.

Randy...

I was raised in a Christian, church-going home. However, early in my high school years, I felt adrift and unanchored. That brought me to some questions I had been dodging for a couple of years: Is there a God? Is He who the Bible says He was? If so, does it really make sense *not* to pledge your life to Him and pursue Him with your whole heart?

So, I soon heard myself praying something like…

God, I have to be honest and tell you that right now, I'm not sure You're even there to hear this prayer. But if You are, I want to ask You to reveal Yourself to me in some way. I genuinely want to know. Because if You are the God I read about in the Bible, I want to give You my future to shape as You see fit, and I want to live completely sold out to You every day.

After that, I said, *Amen*, and went to sleep.

Later, I was awakened in the night with lyrics and a melody going through my mind. I quickly got out of bed, grabbed my guitar, and as fast as I could write, I found myself composing a song. It just flowed onto the page. And it was a surprisingly poetic, melodic, catchy, and yet *deep* song.

The experience seemed so natural and completely unlike anything I had ever experienced. But more than anything else, it confirmed for me that there indeed was a God in heaven and that He had heard and answered a teenage boy's prayer that night.

You see, I had a secret desire to write music. But I had not told anyone about this because every attempt I had made to compose something, even approximating a song, had ended in absolute disaster. So, when I had this experience following my honest prayer, three things were immediately and absolutely clear to me about God:

- He was truly there.
- He knew the deepest desires of my heart.
- He had the power to do wondrous things in and through my life.

My life was never the same again. There was no turning back for me. I was a *goner* for God from that day on.

Why am I telling you all this? Because this is the testimony of how I experienced the baptism in the Holy Spirit.

I didn't know what to call it then. I didn't even believe it could happen. The church I was raised in taught me that after the outpouring of the Holy Spirit on the Day of Pentecost **Acts 2:1-4**, Holy Spirit baptism was experienced at a person's point of salvation. And since I had come to Christ as a young child, I hadn't anticipated having any additional experience with the Holy Spirit.

But whether or not I knew the theology behind what had happened, God knew what I needed and arranged for this young man with a hungry heart to have a *coming upon* experience with the third person of the Trinity. And it changed my life's trajectory in much the same way Pentecost changed the lives of those who comprised the early church.

My heart swelled with passion for God, and I immediately experienced greater boldness in sharing my faith with others. But a couple of years would pass before I began to develop the theological framework for understanding what had happened to me.

Almost immediately after that bedroom baptism, I formed a band with other Christian musicians out of a desire to share the Gospel through the songs we were writing about our relationships with Jesus. We would sing our songs anywhere people would listen: Churches, coffeehouses, parks, beaches, campgrounds, concert halls, or school campuses.

One night after performing a concert at a church, our band was invited to be part of an *afterglow* service that was about to start in another part of the church campus. Curious, I went.

What I experienced at that meeting was new to me – a group of high school and college students praying for other young people who were there to be baptized in the Holy Spirit. I witnessed a room full of people seeking and experiencing a relationship with Jesus that looked more like what I had read about in the New Testament than what I was used to seeing. And I was hooked.

When I got home, I decided to begin studying the book of Acts for myself and see if I could square what I had seen and heard that night with what the scriptures teach.

After several days of this quest, I realized that Jesus was pretty clear in His instructions to His first followers that they *needed* to be filled with the Holy Spirit if they were going to be able to experience the life He was calling them to. And it also became clear to me that He never rescinded those instructions. I also saw that the New Testament pattern was that people received this baptism in the Holy Spirit subsequent to salvation. That's when it dawned on me that this was what I had experienced in my room that night of prayer without knowing what to ask for.

As I continued my study of the early church in the book of Acts, a question began forming in my mind and heart: What's the deal with this business of *speaking in tongues?* I kept encountering it in connection to Spirit baptism. I wanted to know what it was and if it was something I should expect to experience myself.

As I searched the New Testament, I discovered that tongues is a gift from the Holy Spirit that enables enhanced prayer and worship. It is a means for communicating directly from my heart to God without constricting that communication by the limitations of my vocabulary.

My scripture search also revealed that this gift is clearly linked to the experience of being baptized in the Holy Spirit. On three of the five occasions when people were Spirit-baptized in the book of Acts, it is specifically recorded that they spoke in tongues. And a strong case can be made for the other two occasions based on the immediate scriptural contexts and related passages.

So now that I had an answer to my initial question, I longingly asked another: How can I experience this in my life?

I had already become convinced that this was something Jesus meant to be part of a Spirit-baptized believer's life, so I turned to Him in prayer and asked Him to help me. Then I stood, turned my face heavenward, opened my mouth, and waited. I fully expected that the Holy Spirit would somehow grab my tongue and supernaturally move it so that I would start speaking words in a foreign language.

But nothing happened.

I was very disappointed, but I wasn't willing to give up. So, I went back to the scriptures. And as I reread those passages, it dawned on me that the Holy Spirit provided the words while the people did the speaking. That helped me understand that this experience resulted from a partnership between the Spirit of God and me.

I gave it another shot. This time, I prayerfully came before the Lord, opened my mouth, and determined *I would speak* whatever sounds the Holy Spirit would give me. I heard myself making sounds assembled together in a way that seemed like a phrase or sentence in a foreign language.

That's when I encountered what I call the *intellectual bottleneck*.

It was similar to when Peter stepped out of the boat at Jesus' invitation to walk on water. After a few steps, He began to analyze what was happening intellectually. The more he convinced himself of the impossibility of walking on water, the more he sank.

And I found myself sinking.

I began analyzing my experience and found myself discounting its validity. I convinced myself that the sounds I had made were just gibberish. And I was about ready to give up on the whole thing when I sensed the Lord was speaking lovingly but firmly to my heart.

He helped me see that what I was doing was like returning a gift He had given me and asking for something better. It was as though I was rejecting a blessing from my Savior because I didn't like the way it sounded and was asking for something more authentic.

That stopped me cold.

I decided then and there to repent of my intellectualizing and humbly thank Him for the beautiful gift He had graced me with. And I determined to pray that short phrase in tongues as often as I felt prompted by the Spirit. Over the following days and weeks, that turned out to be quite often.

But an interesting thing happened.

The more I spoke in tongues, the less I thought about what I was saying or how it sounded. I found myself just caught up in the act of praying and worshipping from my heart. And one day, it dawned on me that my Spirit-gifted vocabulary was no longer limited to a single phrase. It had blossomed into a broad language without me even being aware of it.

Many years have passed since the experiences I've just described, and they have become so integrated into my Christian life that it seems odd to separate them for discussion, as I have in the above paragraphs. The baptism in the Holy Spirit that Jesus administered to me alone in my bedroom all those years ago and the gift of tongues that has so immeasurably expanded my prayer and worship life are essential aspects of my relationship with Jesus. It is my prayer that if they are not yet essential for you, my testimony may encourage you to *seek and find* **Luke 11:9-13**.

Rachael...

*Author's note: I met Rachael at a women's retreat where I was sharing. I was also asked to give an optional afternoon session regarding the baptism in the Holy Spirit.

The previous year, at our church women's retreat, I had a horrible experience that left a terrible taste in my mouth. The speaker literally forced our group of one hundred women to speak in tongues, trying to *teach* us how to be baptized in the Spirit. I came from a Baptist upbringing, so you might understand how shocked, angry, frustrated, scared, and alone I felt. I spoke with our pastor's wife but still felt very unsettled by the whole experience.

Ironically, two months later, my husband experienced the baptism with the Spirit in the presence of his mentor and our head pastor after a worship service. Wow, really, God? Not only did I have to deal with this at the women's retreat, but now I have to smile and pretend I understand this whole thing with my husband.

A year later, still feeling a sense of fear toward the whole Holy Spirit baptism experience, the speaker was excellent, and everything was going great until she started talking about it. Every fiber of my being is now on HIGH alert. *Not again,* I think to myself, but I realize this isn't the same. She is actually explaining it, and to my surprise, I understand it. My heart starts to race. *Oh, dear Lord, please not here. I can't! I can't do this here!!!*

The service ended, and Sue asked if there was anyone who felt called to stay and pray. Nope, I do NOT want to stay, but why doesn't my heart stop racing? My whole body feels like it's going to explode. I lock eyes with one of the pastors. She asks if I'm ok. I answer *I don't know what to do. I can't be here right now. I know God is calling me to something, but this feels so much more private than this.* Without hesitation, she grabbed my arm, saying, *Go to your room now.*

Almost running, I headed to my room. My heart was racing faster and faster. My eyes were welling with tears. I begged God; *I need my space, Lord! Please just let me get to my room.*

I fumbled with the keys, the door burst open, and I fell on my bed in tears, weeping deep into my pillow. I began to pray, *Ok, yes, Lord, I'm ready. Fill me, consume me. I'm yours.* I repeated this prayer through tears, drool, and snot, but my heart is *HIS.* My prayer turned to wailing deep into my pillow, but I was alone with my Savior, so I couldn't care less about the crazy tears.

Not to my surprise, my wailing and tears began forming words. Words I didn't understand came from a deep well within my soul I've never been able to express. I continued to allow my soul to pour out for what seemed like hours. I'm tired, and my eyes are swollen. I hear, *Rest in Me.* I fell asleep almost immediately.

I woke up two hours later, startled by the time that had passed. I jumped up and ran downstairs to take over an event where I was scheduled to help.

Before I even got to the last step, Satan attacked me full force! *You idiot! You fell for all those superficial emotions! What would your mom say? She warned you about this. SHAME!!! I thought you were smarter than all of this!*
Feeling alone, ashamed, embarrassed, and extremely confused, I sat on the bottom step. My mentor saw me and asked me what was wrong. I told her my story. Instantly she squealed with delight and joy for me, but she saw my hurt and confusion. She sat next to me and prayed. Her prayer was full of everything I was feeling. I wanted more than anything to sit up from that prayer and be just fine, but I wasn't.

That night at the last service, the Holy Spirit was moving in women's hearts like crazy, but I felt distant from it all. My mind was full of doubt and self-criticism for what I had just experienced. But I sat quietly watching women falling to their knees, some hurting and needing healing, and some ready to let God into a place in their life they had been holding back (like myself). Some were experiencing God's love for the first time. I heard His voice, *It's time, Rachael. Go pray with them. Use your gifts. I will lead you.*

I knelt down next to the closest woman to me, and God spoke to me. He led me in a prayer I never could have come up with on my own, and He continued to help me through each prayer as I prayed for other women. I felt Him confirming what He had done for me in that little room. As I crawled around that concrete floor praying over many women, I knew without a doubt that the events He laid out for me were in His will.

My Savior, in His amazing love, grace, patience, and incredible gentle nature, led me to a private room where the He Holy Spirit baptized me!

Christopher...

One of the most significant and life-changing experiences I remember was a mission trip to Australia when I was nineteen. Every morning, our team would gather to pray and do our devotionals together. I had just recommitted myself to Jesus a year prior before entering college. I had trusted Him for salvation when I was a freshman in high school, but over the years, I had gone back to worldly living and not living in the fullness of His Spirit.

Back to my trip to Australia...

We were praying together as a team, and I was spontaneously baptized in the Holy Spirit and started to speak in tongues. I remembered what Jesus said in Acts when He told His disciples, *You will receive power from on high to be my witnesses in Jerusalem, Judea, Samaria, and to the ends of the earth,* **Luke 24:49**. It was an incredible experience, although it was not an emotional one for me in that moment. However, I knew Jesus had filled my cup, and I was overflowing with the power of the Holy Spirit!

The rest of my mission trip to Australia was something I could have never expected! As my team placed fliers into mailboxes for one of our outreach events, the Holy Spirit gave me prophetic words for many of the households I was passing. I knew that God was walking with me. At one point, while our team conducted evangelism in various high schools, the Holy Spirit led me to pray for someone with a broken finger, and God healed him!

My experience with the baptism of the Holy Spirit continued when I came home. Since that time, I've had a deeper intimacy with God in prayer, and the Holy Spirit has been illuminating the truths of the Bible in ways I've never understood before.

Now, I can't imagine my life without the power of the Holy Spirit that comes through Spirit baptism. When I think about the Spirit-filled life, I can characterize it with comfort, joy, and power. Many times, I haven't known how to pray for myself or others because of confusing and challenging situations. Still, the Spirit's intercession through my spiritual language has brought truth and guidance in those situations. I can always rely on the gift of tongues to comfort myself and others when there is a need.

I have never before experienced the kind of joy that the Holy Spirit has produced in me. Before in my life, my joy and happiness depended on my circumstances and how I felt. The Holy Spirit produces a joy within me that doesn't ride on external matters but solely on the person of Christ, who I can always rejoice in.

Lastly, I know from personal experience that the power given to us by the Holy Spirit is needed to testify to the life and salvation found only in Jesus Christ. His overflow has given me confidence and boldness to preach the crucified and risen Christ, not caring about the fear or praises of man.

Ruthie...

In the past, I was vaguely aware of the Holy Spirit in my life. Nevertheless, for many years I attended a Christian church that believed that the gifts of the Spirit were only needed during biblical times, and we didn't need these gifts today.

When we started the *Pneuma Life Bible Study*, the Lord was healing and restoring me. The Lord revealed Himself to me. He showed me the Father who loves me unconditionally, the Son who forgives my sins and washes me clean, and the Holy Spirit who helps me, guides me, and draws me closer to Him. The *Pneuma Life Study* took us through the Holy Spirit's presence in Genesis to Jesus' return in the power of the Spirit, to the gifts of the Spirit.

I was so filled with the Holy Spirit that I desired the gift of speaking in tongues. However, did I want to be one of those crazy people whose unrecognizable banter made the world raise their eyebrows and wrinkle their noses? Yes, I did! I wanted the Holy Spirit to move through my life continually.

Over the course of our study, Sue shared that my spiritual language might only begin with one or two syllables. So, I went home and asked the Holy Spirit to give me this gift, to speak His prayer through me. I began with *aaaah* and nothing. The attempts were many, but I had faith and let the Holy Spirit grow my desire. Then one morning, as I was getting ready for work, putting on my mascara, I spoke, *aaaah....aaah....aaah....abba desta ramallah...* and the prayer went on. I stopped what I was doing and let the Holy Spirit speak through me. I felt so close to the Lord.

Here is an email I sent to those in our *Pneuma Life* group:

> *Hi There,*
> *I just have to share...*
> *First of all, I somehow got the idea to listen to myself as I prayed my prayer language. However, I didn't concentrate on that idea much because it felt like I was being distracted by it, and I didn't want to interrupt my prayer. But it came to me as I listened to myself: I can control this language; stop and start as I feel led by the Holy Spirit.*
>
> *Do you remember the words of my prayer language I shared with you? They were 'ramala abba desta.' I just sensed that I was to look up these words online. It turns out that Ramallah is a town six miles north of Jerusalem and is mainly inhabited by Christian Arabs. The term is Arabic for 'Height of God.' We all know that 'abba' means father. And 'desta'? It means joy. Tears welled up in my eyes.*
>
> *On another note, I asked the Holy Spirit to pray what needed prayer most. He knows there are more important things to pray about than what is right under my nose. So, the Holy Spirit prayed and prayed through me. I want you to know that even though I didn't know what I was saying, I felt like, wow, there is so much to pray about, and I couldn't cover it all on my own. What a release to know I was praying beyond what I personally know. All in all, my prayer felt more thorough and more complete.*

The greatest benefit of this gift and more of the Holy Spirit has been enjoying a more intimate relationship with the Lord. The Holy Spirit helps me to see Jesus every day. He causes me to see my sinful nature and who I truly am, and He is transforming me more and more into the image of the Savior.

Mike...

Having grown up in a Pentecostal denomination with an emphasis on the baptism of the Holy Spirit, the subject of the Holy Spirit has never been foreign to me. However, attention was primarily on the *experience* of the event instead of the purpose and the promise of the Spirit's power.

Because of the extreme emotionalism I had seen, I grew up with the misconception that Spirit baptism was more of a possession than infilling or an overflow. I thought He took over and made you shake, talk in another language, and act crazy! Being extremely introverted, this scared me to death. It kept me from wanting or even desiring something that somehow would alter my personality or push me beyond a comfortable response to his presence.

When I was eleven, our church had weeklong meetings with a visiting evangelist. After each of his messages, he invited those of us who would like to receive the baptism with the Holy Spirit and our prayer language to come to the front of the meeting. I sheepishly stepped forward in tremendous anguish over what would happen next. I was instructed to lift my hands and begin to say the name of Jesus over and over, faster and faster. After about 10 minutes of being tongue-tied, embarrassed, and frustrated, I gave up. The sad fact is that I thought something was wrong with me. I thought I had offended God, grieved the Holy Spirit, had unconfessed sin, or simply didn't do the *formula* correctly. I completely gave up.

Three months later, while preoccupied with something else, a thought came out of nowhere, *ask me.* I knew immediately in my heart what that meant. I prayed, *Jesus, I want to be filled with the power of your Holy Spirit.* As I got those words out, I realized I was no longer praying in English. What had seemed impossible for me earlier was made a reality by the Holy Spirit.

Now, these many years later, I have been in full-time pastoral ministry, leading others in God's Word, his love, and the power of the Holy Spirit in a believer's life.

Vivian...

Through a *Pneuma Life* study at my church, I came to know about the Holy Spirit. However, as a new believer, I was apprehensive about His work in my life because I lacked confidence and did not feel certain about my salvation. The most challenging obstacle I had to overcome was forgiving myself for my past since I didn't feel worthy of God's grace and mercy. Because of all His blessings throughout my life, I questioned Him why He was so wonderful to me when I was so broken emotionally and spiritually. I was ashamed of having so much when others were more worthy than me.

Yet, His Word comforted me:

> *For if our heart condemns us, God is greater than our heart,*
> *and knows all things.*
> **1 John 3:20**

My prayer language came shortly after a *Pneuma Life* session, where the topic was speaking in tongues. *And they were all filled with the Holy Spirit and began to speak with tongues, as the Spirit gave them utterance,* **Acts 2:4.** I remember telling myself that I wasn't *seasoned* enough as a Christian, so it would be a long time before I would utter anything other than English.

A few days passed, and the Holy Spirit caught my attention as I was commuting home from work one afternoon. He prompted me with two words: *Just try!* **Luke 12:12** came to my mind: *For the Holy Spirit will teach you in that very hour what you ought to say.*

The first few sounds I heard were nothing I could even begin to compose or make sense of. However, once I got going, it wasn't what I heard with my ears—but what I heard and felt in my heart. Just an outpouring of praise to God about everything and everyone in my life, followed by asking for forgiveness for every action, word, or thought that was not pleasing to Him. I found myself praying for people I hadn't even thought of praying for—my heart cried out to the Lord that His grace would touch their lives as He had done mine.

But God has revealed them to us through His Spirit. For the Spirit searches all things, yes, the deep things of God. For what man knows the things of a man except the spirit of the man which is in him? Even so no one knows the things of God except the Spirit of God.
1 Corinthians 2:10-11

Consciously, I wanted to stop since I was scaring myself and the thought crossed my mind that I had now completely *gone over the edge!* Eventually, I sensed my time of prayer coming to a close. It was then I realized how much serenity and peace of mind I was experiencing.

I have continued to grow in the Lord. When I am impatient and not waiting on Him, the Holy Spirit is kind yet firm in reminding me I have confidence in my salvation and can stand unashamed before Him. In moments of uncertainty and anxiousness, the Holy Spirit calms me when I want to run, hide, or, worse yet, take matters into my own hands. Through the Holy Spirit, in times of solitude or loneliness, even in a crowded room, I hear His voice, *You are never alone.*

Recommended Reading...

NOTE: These resources have been an encouragement and blessing to my life although I might not completely agree with all the authors share.

The Holy Spirit and You – Dennis and Rita Bennett

The Beauty of Spiritual Language – Jack Hayford, Litt.D.

The Promise of the Father – Dr. Steve Schell

Holy Spirit: Are We Flammable or Fireproof? – Reinhard Bonke

The Spirit of the Lord is Upon Us – Dr. Leslie Keegel

Victorious Spiritual Warfare, So Simple, Grandma Can Do It – Maureen Broderson

Your Battles Belong to the Lord – Joyce Meyer

Healing the Sick: A Divine Healing Classic – T.L. Osborne

Forgotten God – Francis Chan

Help is Here – Max Lucado

Expecting Miracles – Heidi and Rolland Baker

The Spirit Bade Me Go – David Du Plessis

Intimate Friendship with God – Joy Dawson

Chasing the Dragon – Jackie Pullinger

Draw the Circle: The Forty Day Prayer Challenge – Mark Batterson

Building a Firm Foundation – Sue Boldt

New Spirit Filled Life Bible – Jack W. Hayford, Litt.D.

Key Word Study Bible – Dr. Spiros Zodhiates

Foundations of Pentecostal Theology – Guy P. Duffield & Nathaniel M. Van Cleave

Made in the USA
Middletown, DE
11 September 2023

38344233R00126